COVERING

Your

LIFE

in

PRAYER

ERWIN W. LUTZER

HARVEST HOUSE PUBLISHERS
EUGENE, OREGON

Cover by Dugan Design Group, Bloomington, Minnesota

Cover photo © iStockphoto / ChrisHepburn

COVERING YOUR LIFE IN PRAYER
Copyright © 2013 by Erwin W. Lutzer
Published by Harvest House Publishers
Eugene, Oregon 97402
www.harvesthousepublishers.com

Library of Congress Cataloging-in-Publication Data

Lutzer, Erwin W.
  Covering your life in prayer/Erwin W. Lutzer.
    pages cm
  ISBN 978-0-7369-5327-6 (pbk.)
  ISBN 978-0-7369-5328-3 (eBook)
    1. Prayer—Christianity. 2. Bible—Prayers. 3. Bible—Devotional use. I. Title.
  BV210.3.L88 2013
  248.3'2--dc23

2013000621

To my lovely wife, Rebecca,
who covers my life and that of our extended family
with regular, believing prayer.
"Her children rise up and call her blessed;
her husband also, he praises her:
'Many women have done excellently,
but you surpass them all'" (Proverbs 31:28-29).

Contents

Praying from the Abundant Riches of Scripture

Often when we pray for others, we either fall into meaningless repetition, or submit a grocery list of requests to God, hoping that He'll respond to our wishes and desires. When we've finished praying, we end up being unsatisfied, fretful, and uncertain as to whether or not we can trust God with the assignment we've just given Him.

My personal experience has been that such "need-based" praying is often boring, filled with uncertainty, and reduces prayer to a meaningless exercise.

What if we changed our perspective on prayer and began to pray Scripture? What if we echoed back to God that which we know is His will? Wouldn't that stimulate our faith, bring glory to Him, and rid us of the repetition that Jesus warned us about when He said, "When you are praying, do not use meaningless repetition"(Matthew 6:7)?

Years ago I discovered that when I pray Scripture, I anticipate my time of prayer with excitement, wondering exactly what I would pray next. Best of all, praying in this way sinks deep roots into God's promises and His will. Such prayer is effective not just in moving God's heart toward us, but in giving us a deep and settled satisfaction of knowing that we've just connected with our heavenly Father.

Will you join me in praying Scripture for ourselves and others?

God has blessed Rebecca and me with eight lovely and lively grandchildren. Long ago I gave up on the idea of simply listing their names before God and asking Him to "bless" them. What I've chosen to do is pray for each one of them one day a week beginning from the eldest to the youngest (I pray for two on Saturday!). And each week I choose a passage of Scripture to pray on their behalf. In other words, I use the same passage for each child, but adapt it to their needs and ages. So while I pray the same verse each day of the week, I'll adapt the passage for each child individually—mentioning other concerns and requests in the process, yet keeping the Scripture passage as the core of the prayer.

I encourage you to do the same for your children, your spouse, your friends, and for yourself. As you do, you'll discover in the course of time that you are praying for both your and their spiritual and material needs. Of course I hope that whole families can unite around these passages and pray them. I encourage you to choose seven (or more) people for whom you'll pray each as you follow along on this prayer journey.

Praying the same verse for various people during the week should in no way exhaust the praying you should do each day. Rather, this will help you get started on a journey that I hope will last a lifetime. An added benefit is that you'll probably have memorized the verses by the time the week is over!

Throughout the next 52 weeks, we will alternate between the Old and New Testaments as we pray passages of Scripture. The beauty of praying in this manner is that there is an abundance of promises, prayers, and verses all through the Bible that can be adapted for prayer. What I present in this book is only a sampling of the vast resources of Scripture.

Are you ready to begin?

Spread out your petition before God, and then say,
"Thy will, not mine, be done."
The sweetest lesson I have learned in God's school
is to let the Lord choose for me.

D.L. Moody

A Prayer Against Fear and Greed

*"After these things the word of the LORD came to
Abram in a vision: 'Fear not, Abram, I am your shield;
your reward shall be very great.'"*

—GENESIS 15:1

Let's understand the importance of this promise! Four powerful kings of the north plundered the five kings of the south (near the Dead Sea) and carried off all the treasures of the kings of Sodom and Gomorrah.

When Abraham learned that Lot was among the captives, he rallied 318 troops and pursued the attackers all the way north to Dan (about 140 miles!). Then he continued his pursuit all the way to Hobah (another 100 miles!). In a night attack, he rescued the plundered possessions as well as the frightened captives—Lot among them.

As for the king of Sodom, he was so grateful to Abraham for bravely rescuing the people from his city that he wanted only his people returned to him. As for the possessions, Abraham could keep them for himself. But Abraham refused this offer, saying he didn't want the king of Sodom to be able to say that he made Abraham rich. Abraham was trusting God alone for any wealth he might receive.

This leads us to the promise of Genesis 15:1: "Fear not, Abram, I am your shield; your reward shall be very great."

God gave these words to Abraham because: (1) Abraham might be tempted to live in fear that the kings he'd defeated might retaliate and organize a raid against him. Furthermore, (2) Abraham had just said no to a great deal of wealth that could have legitimately been his. God said that He would reward Abraham.

Indeed, the Lord Himself would be Abraham's reward. What an encouragement these words were!

Let's take the promise God gave Abraham and adapt it as a prayer for someone we love—someone who is experiencing a time of doubt and fear. And let us pray it for ourselves too.

A Prayer to Begin Your Time of Intercession

Father, I pray today for _____. I pray that You'll be a shield to them, protecting them spiritually and physically. Let no evil person do harm against them. Also, personally, guard their emotions from the enemies of fear and doubt. I pray that they will rest in Your promise of protection and that their hearts will be filled with a quiet confidence that You are with them, beside them. Help them to flee to You as their refuge and strength. Replace fear with trust and peace.

Also, I pray that they might be kept from the greed that would spoil their relationship with You. Like Abraham, protect them from foolish "get rich quick" schemes or using deceit to earning money. Above all, let us be motivated to seek Your face and not just ask for blessings from Your hand. Let us all be faithful and content with You as our great reward.

I pray in the powerful name of Jesus, Amen.

A Prayer for God's Presence in the Midst of Injustice

"Joseph's master took him and put him into the prison, the place where the king's prisoners were confined, and he was there in prison. But the LORD was with Joseph and showed him stead-fast love and gave him favor in the sight of the keeper of the prison... The keeper of the prison paid no attention to anything that was in Joseph's charge, because the LORD was with him. And whatever he did, the LORD made it succeed."

—GENESIS 39:20-21,23

Think of the significance of this remarkable account.

Joseph is imprisoned, based on a false accusation. Potiphar's wife tried to lure him into sexual sin, and when he refused, she scorned him and had her husband throw him in jail.

Yet God displayed His grace to Joseph even as he was incarcerated in a primitive, harsh dungeon. God was with Joseph when he was exalted in Egypt, and here, we see God with Joseph to bless him even in the darkness of the cavern—with his feet in shackles and his neck in irons (Psalm 105:17-18).

God is with us in our promotions and our demotions; He is with us when we are hired and when we are fired, when our salary is increased and when it is decreased. God walks with us through times of blessing and injustice, exhilaration and sorrow.

Life can be cruel, and even our friends can be ready to betray us. And, in this litigious society, truth is twisted and frivolous lawsuits are often filed with the worst of intentions. Like Joseph, we must maintain our integrity with the sure confidence that God is watching, orchestrating and caring for us.

God uses injustice in the lives of His children. He does not leave us when everyone else does. He knows both sides of every story. Best of all,

He even knows the hidden motives of every heart. Our friends might not understand; our enemies will intentionally distort, malign, and slander without cause. But God knows all and assures us that vengeance belongs to Him.

As far as Joseph was concerned, he had no reason to believe that he would ever get out of prison. He had no attorney to represent him; there were no laws to which he could appeal. He was stripped of his dignity, reputation, and rights. Yet God had a surprise for Joseph. One morning he was whisked out of the cell to interpret pharaoh's dream, and before he knew it, he was riding on a chariot, second in command to the pharaoh himself.

God might also surprise us by delivering us from false accusations. Meanwhile, if we continue to find ourselves the victim of injustice, we can be reminded of the words frequently spoken by Corrie ten Boom: "There is no pit so deep that God's love is not deeper still."

After giving praise to God and yielding yourself to Him, adapt these verses to pray for yourself or a friend when you are distressed by injustices done to you or them.

A Prayer to Begin Your Time of Intercession

Father, I pray today for _____ and ask that You might give them great faith even if unjustly treated; show them steadfast love and favor in the sight of all who know them. Help them to resist sexual sin even as Joseph did. And when mistreated at school or work, help them to remember that they need not avenge themselves because You are the avenger of all wrongs.

Give them such obvious integrity that others might trust them implicitly because they recognize that You are with them. Father, we know that integrity, once lost, is difficult to restore, so help them to resist all temptation that would compromise their moral and spiritual values—even when under pressure. And whatever they do, cause them to succeed in a way that reflects Your glory and favor.

Finally, may we always remember that Your presence is with us, even as You were with Joseph. May this assurance of Your constant presence keep us from sin and loneliness. Help us to enjoy Your company. We pray in Jesus' name, Amen.

A Prayer for the Faith to Forgive

*"Do not fear, for am I in the place of God? As for you, you
meant evil against me, but God meant it for good, to bring it
about that many people should be kept alive, as they are today.
So do not fear; I will provide for you and your little ones."*
—GENESIS 50:19-21

These are incredible words from the lips of Joseph. Twenty years earlier, his brothers had sold him as a slave to a caravan of traders on their way to Egypt. With the death of their father, Jacob, these brothers are afraid they will not be fully reconciled to him. They fear that now that their father is dead, Joseph will retaliate against them to "settle the score" in response to the humiliation and pain they inflicted on him so many years earlier.

What makes Joseph's response so remarkable is that he sees in his injustice the sovereignty of God. His experience in the prison (referred to in last week's prayer) helped him to see that evil itself can be part of God's plan. And although this in no way absolved his brothers of responsibility for their betrayal of him, the fact is that God is greater than the evil that others do to us!

My experience has been that if all that we see is the devil in the evil done against us, we will be led to despair. But if we remember to quote Martin Luther, "that even the devil is God's devil," we will be able to see that God has a plan for us, and that He can use evil for His purposes, and yes, for our good!

Joseph, therefore, felt free to forgive his brothers. And he even proved his forgiveness by taking care of them!

As we pray for ourselves and others this week, let us pray that we'll see God in our afflictions, and that we will be able to lay down bitterness. "See to it that no one fails to obtain the grace of God; that no 'root of bitterness' springs up and causes trouble, and by it many become defiled" (Hebrews 12:15). Note that (1) bitterness has roots, and (2) the poison of bitterness affects others.

A Prayer to Begin Your Time of Intercession

Father, help us, like Joseph, to see that we must be willing to be reconciled to those who have wronged us. Give us the faith to believe that even evil can be used for good if we are willing to submit to You, to let go of our bitterness.

I pray for _____ and ask that they might be willing to trust Your grace in the midst of the pain, abuse, insensitivity, and injustice. I pray that they would be able to let go of the bitterness and pain and anger. Help them to believe that what others meant for evil, You meant for good. Release them from the negative effects of their past, I pray.

I ask that You break Satan's stronghold of anger, revenge, and victimization that is so much a part of our experience. Bring us all to the light of Your grace for our past, and may we move on to a life of freedom, leaving the chains of anger and bitterness in the past.

In Jesus' name, Amen.

A Prayer for Patience to Let God Do His Work

"Fear not, stand firm, and see the salvation of the LORD,
which he will work for you today... The LORD will fight for you,
and you have only to be silent."

—EXODUS 14:13-14

Pharaoh has finally let the Israelites leave Egypt after the firstborn sons of that nation were put to death by the Angel of the Lord. Now that the waters of the Red Sea have parted for them to walk though, they see the Egyptian army pursuing them in their chariots, intending to capture the Israelites and return them to slavery, or worse. The Israelites are terrified and God gives Moses this promise that He will fight on their behalf.

Passages like this raise the question of exactly how specific promises given in a particular Old Testament situation apply to us. Obviously, there are times when we must fight and not simply remain silent in order to see the salvation of the Lord. In biblical times, God gave specific instructions for specific situations. Here He asked Moses to be quiet; in contrast, later He will tell Joshua and all the people to march around Jericho and shout at an appointed time.

However, the basic principle of the above verse applies to us as New Testament believers: *God stands with us, ready to defend us if only we will acknowledge His presence and trust Him to do what we cannot.* Our human nature wants to rush to our defense, and while that might be wise in certain situations, God often has a different time table and we must wait on Him to come to our rescue.

Keep in mind that it was God who led the Israelites to this impasse in the desert. God led them into a tight place to prove that He was adequate for even the most perilous predicament. Just so, God often leads us into situations where human resources are no match to our desperate need. Either God comes through for us or we falter; either God fights on our behalf or we are overcome.

Was it not St. Francis of Assisi who prayed, "Lord, help me to change the things I can, to accept those things I cannot, and the wisdom to know the difference!"? We must trust God to change the things we cannot. In the nick of time God came through for Israel, and He can and will do the same for us.

A Prayer to Begin Your Time of Intercession

Father, let us be quiet in Your presence long enough to see You fight on our behalf. I pray for _____, that they might trust You to go before them, to work out situations and problems where there appear to be no good options. Help us to know when to act and when to wait, when to shout and when to stand still. Come to us and win victories in our personal lives, and in all our relationships. Help us to submit until we are willing to be patient and wait for You to resolve difficulties that are beyond us to remedy.

I pray that _____ might not lash out and fight their battles out of fear, anger, or resentment, but that they will take the time to submit to Your timing. May they believe that You care and will come to aid all those who wait before You.

In Jesus' name, Amen.

A Prayer for the Glory of God

"Please show me your glory."
—EXODUS 33:18

Imagine what this short prayer means! The children of Israel were delayed in their journey because of idolatry. While Moses was on Mount Sinai, the people made a golden calf so they could have a "god" like the other nations around them. God was very angry, and Moses—bless him—threw down the stone tablets that were written by the finger of God. After confronting the people about their sin, the perpetrators were put to death.

Moving forward, God made this suggestion: that His presence—the fire during the night and the cloud during the day—would no longer accompany them, lest the next time He "consume" them. In His stead, He would send an angel to guide them.

Moses was bitterly disappointed. After all, the presence of the Almighty was what distinguished the Israelites from all the other nations of the world. Moses said that if the presence of God did not go with them, he did not want to go. Better to remain in the wilderness with the presence of God than to go to the Promised Land without Him! No place can satisfy without God; no wealth can satisfy without God; no pleasure can satisfy without God. Better to be in the desert with God than to experience the bounty of Canaan without His presence! So, in answer to Moses' prayer, God gave the assurance that indeed, He would go with them. The divine presence would return.

Moses was still dissatisfied. Although he had spent days on the mountain with God, he still craved to see more of God, to experience Him more fully. He prayed that he would see God's glory. In effect, he prayed, "God, show me as much of You as I can take!"

Of course, to see God directly would be like standing next to the sun. So God accommodated Himself to Moses by asking him to go into a cleft of rock, and as His glory passed by, Moses would catch at least a glimpse of the divine presence. God would satisfy Moses' desire and reaffirm His promise to accompany the people into the Land.

Now, what has Moses been doing in heaven since his arrival so many ages ago? We don't know the details, but we do know that centuries after his death he appeared on the Mount of Transfiguration, enjoying once again the glory of God, only this time along with Elijah. This reminds us that throughout all of eternity, we will rejoice in seeing God face to face; we will at last be in His presence to behold the divine glory without interruption. Moses could not exhaust the wonder of God's glory, and neither will we be able to.

Although in this life we should not expect to see the glory of God physically as Moses did, we must pray that we would share Moses' passionate desire for the glory of God. After all, nothing else really matters except that God be glorified in our lives. And, if we focus on God's glory, our lives are simplified and our goals clarified.

Let us pray that the passion Moses had would be ours as well.

A Prayer to Begin Your Time of Intercession

Heavenly Father, give me the heart of Moses, who cared only to see Your glory. Help me to get to know You as well as it is possible for sinners to know You in this life. Today, show me Your glory through Your Word and help me to reflect this glory to others. Let me be like Moses, who did not know that his face shone—let me live in Your presence and radiate Your presence to others.

And I pray for _____, that they might so strongly desire to know You that they would be willing to sacrifice time and energy just to be assured that You are pleased with them. Above all, give them a holy desire to glorify You in their private lives, in their public lives, and in all their associations. May You be their most prized treasure. I pray You will get glory from their lives.

Consume us with a desire to see You glorified in our lives. Show us Your glory!

We pray in Jesus' name, Amen.

Note: Every morning before I get out of bed I pray, "Lord, glorify Yourself today at my expense!" Join me in making that your habit too, for nothing else really matters except that God get glory from our lives. This is the best way to simplify our lives around one unifying passion. *Do it, Lord!*

A Prayer to Die to Self-Will

*"Truly, truly, I say to you, unless a grain of wheat falls into the
earth and dies, it remains alone; but if it dies, it bears much
fruit. Whoever loves his life loses it, and whoever hates his life in
this world will keep it for eternal life."*

—John 12:24-25

When Satan rebelled, there were now two "wills" in the universe.
From now on, one of God's creatures would oppose the
Almighty—unsuccessfully, to be sure—in all that he would do. And a
drop of Satan's rebellion has fallen on every human heart. If we expect
to be mightily used by God, there must come a time when we "die to
self" as the saying goes. This means that we are no longer driven by
our reputations, our successes, or by our possessions. Only one thing
matters: God and His glory.

Just imagine: All jealousy ends, all complaining ends, and we no
longer compete with others because we want to "show them a thing or
two"! We are content with where God has placed us, and we no longer
strive to be recognized, praised, or admired.

This dying to self is both an act and a process. Or, perhaps more
accurately, it happens through many acts of dedication and surrender. We come to a point where we no longer fight with God and chafe
under His mighty hand.

In the pyramids in Egypt, archaeologists found grain that had been
lying in dry darkness for thousands of years. The grain grew when put
into soil with water and sunshine! The life was present in the kernels for
thousands of years, but they remained dormant and could not bear fruit
because they had not "died." Jesus wants us to "fall into the soil" and "die,"
so to speak, so that the life of the Holy Spirit can break forth within us.

The result? Jesus said, "We will bear much fruit."

A Prayer to Begin Your Time of Intercession

Father, I pray that I might finally come to the end of self-rule. I confess that I am driven by the need for the approval of others, the need to be recognized, and the need to assert myself for my own good and self-aggrandizement. Today, I lay all that at Your feet and pray that I might die to my own self-generated plans; may only Yours matter.

I also pray for _____ and ask that they might be brought in submission before You. I pray that You will bring circumstances into their lives that will force them to lay down the weapons of a rebel and submit to Your authority and lordship. Like a seed with no agenda of its own, may they be willing to die and let You grow them for Your glory and honor.

In Jesus' name, Amen.

A Prayer for Personal Peace

"Peace I leave with you; my peace I give to you.
Not as the world gives do I give to you. Let not your hearts be
troubled, neither let them be afraid."

—JOHN 14:27

As you read that passage, keep in mind the context of Jesus' promise. He had just told His disciples that He was about to go away, leaving them on this earth while He returned to His Father. The disciples were devastated and confused. After all, as long as Jesus was with them, He would take care of every situation as it developed: He could quiet storms, provide instant food for multitudes, forgive sins, and heal the sick with a word from His mouth.

Now He was leaving them.

Jesus assured them that He would not leave them alone, but that the Comforter (the Holy Spirit) would take His place. And, despite the loss, they would receive His peace.

Please notice that this peace is a gift. Because it's a gift, it isn't tied to circumstances. It's a gift that's inserted *in the midst* of our circumstances. No matter how bad things become, Jesus can give us the gift of His peace—an unearned gift.

This is a supernatural gift, given by the only One qualified to give it.

Jesus knows your past history. He knows what you're going through, and He also knows what your tomorrows hold. He knows all the contingencies, all the possibilities. He sees your coming promotions and demotions. He already knows when and where you will die, and what will be said at your funeral! He can bring peace to us no matter where we are along the continuum of life.

A Prayer to Begin Your Time of Intercession

Father, I begin by praying that I might rest in the peace You have promised to me. Help me to not surrender to the thieves of anger, guilt, anxiety, and depression, for they want to steal this gift from me. I confess any sins that would cause the cup of peace to spring a leak.

And now I pray for _____, asking that You might give them peace. I pray against all the forces arrayed against them that would steal peace from their heart also. I pray that anger and strife might cease in their heart. Help them to receive the power of the Holy Spirit, who is the means by which this peace is brought to us.

Help us to receive the Spirit's power by faith, thanking You in advance that we will receive peace today.

In Jesus' name, Amen.

A Prayer for Fruitfulness

*"Abide in me, and I in you. As the branch cannot bear fruit by
itself, unless it abides in the vine, neither can you, unless you
abide in me...By this my Father is glorified, that you bear much
fruit and so prove to be my disciples. As the Father has loved me,
so have I loved you. Abide in my love."*

—JOHN 15:4,8-9

We should be shocked to realize that Jesus says that if we are not
fruit-bearing Christians, we are really of no use whatever to God!
Even more sobering, He says that if anyone does not bear fruit, he is
"thrown away like a branch and withers; and the branches are gath-
ered, thrown into the fire, and burned" (John 15:6).

Some interpret this to mean that true Christians who stop bearing
fruit can lose their salvation and be burned in the fires of hell. Other
passages, however, teach that those who are truly saved will not be lost
(John 10:28-30). So it's best to understand this to mean that (1) some
branches were never really connected to the vine, or (2) that the fire
refers to the judgment of believers, not the fire of hell. At any rate, let's
not miss the bottom line: *If we do not bear fruit, we are displeasing God.*

The fruit Jesus was speaking about undoubtedly is the fruit of the
Spirit—the qualities of the inner life that bring glory to God: love, joy,
peace, etc. This fruit grows silently within us, but manifests itself in
outward attitudes and behavior.

To *abide* means "to live or dwell." In practical terms it means a
constant and conscious dependence on Christ every day of our lives.
We yield to Christ in the morning, but then repeatedly affirm our
dependence on Him as the day continues. Through such submission
and faith, the Spirit is free to work the supernatural changes He desires
to bring about within our hearts.

Earlier in this book, we prayed that we would die to self. An important part of this process is learning to depend solely upon Christ each day and thus "abide" in His strength and power.

A Prayer to Begin Your Time of Intercession

Father, I pray that You might enable me to "abide in You"—that is, rest in Your provision and love. I pray that I might not only bear fruit, but *much* fruit, for Your glory. May I not be a branch that is barren, a branch that is "thrown into the fire."

And now I pray for _____, that they might come to know You and trust You with their lives and future. I pray that they might see that You are well aware that we cannot change ourselves; You do not expect us to bear fruit by our willpower but by dependence on You and Your blessed Spirit.

Help us to confess every sin that stands in the way of abiding in Your promises. Help us to simply be clean vessels that rest in Your spiritual resources and strength.

In Jesus' name, Amen.

Frequently the richest answers are not the speediest...
A prayer may be all the longer on its voyage
because it is bringing us a heavier freight of blessing.
Delayed answers are not only trials of faith,
but they give us an opportunity of honoring God
by our steadfast confidence in Him under apparent repulses.

C.H. Spurgeon

A Prayer to Be Kept from Evil

"I do not ask that you take them out of the world, but that you keep them from the evil one. They are not of the world, just as I am not of the world. Sanctify them in the truth; your word is truth. And for their sake I consecrate myself, that they also may be sanctified in the truth."

—John 17:15-17,19

M any parents who bolt the door of their house at night nevertheless allow thieves to come into their homes and steal their children's hearts. The body of the child is there, but the heart is being stolen by the television set, cell phones, computers, and other media gadgets. A steady stream of degrading music, various forms of pornography, and violence (often in video games) is ingested into the child's psyche—and we wonder why they don't follow the Lord in their later years.

Jesus prayed that we might be *in* the world but not *of* the world, just as He was. He knew—and we should too—that there is a world out there that is hostile toward God. Elsewhere John defines it as "the desires of the flesh and the desires of the eyes and pride of life" (1 John 2:16). This world, John adds, "is passing away along with its desires, but whoever does the will of God abides forever" (verse 17).

We can't break the addictive power of modern technology and its stream of worldly entertainment without consistent, focused, spiritual warfare. The lust or desire of the flesh, the lure of covetousness, and the pride of possessions and appearance—these fight against God. John said it clearly: "If anyone loves the world, the love of the Father is not in him" (verse 15).

We must pray for ourselves and others that we would be kept from evil.

A Prayer to Begin Your Time of Intercession

Father, I throw myself at Your feet, imploring You to deliver me from both the overt and subtle intrusion of the world into my life. Help me to break with any sinful avenues that I frequently choose, that I might not seek to satisfy my desires apart from Your holiness.

I pray for _____, who is bound in their addiction to television, pornography, and/or violence. Show them that these sins always have a bitter aftertaste, and that although they promise like a god, they pay like the devil. I pray that they might be willing to break with all of the open doors by which the world is invited into their hearts.

But Father, they are bound, slaves to sin; and slaves cannot set themselves free. So come in power to rescue and deliver them.

In faith, I withstand the power of Satan, the "god of this world."

Give me a passion for Jesus that is greater than my passion to sin.

In Jesus' name, Amen.

A Prayer for Spiritual Protection

*"The angel of God who was going before the host of Israel moved
and went behind them, and the pillar of cloud moved from
before them and stood behind them, coming between the host of
Egypt and the host of Israel. And there was the cloud and
the darkness. And it lit up the night without one coming near
the other all night."*

—EXODUS 14:19-20

Think of the drama! The Israelites, two million strong, were trekking toward the wilderness when they found themselves trapped. The Red Sea was ahead of them, the angry Egyptians on chariots were behind them, and there was no possible exit to the right or left. Understandably, they were helpless and terrified. They fully expected to be massacred and have their bodies strewn across the landscape as a witness to Egyptian cruelty and superiority.

But thankfully, the Angel of the Lord did not withdraw in Israel's desperate time of need; rather, the Angel moved to provide protection. The cloud sent to guide them moved to the back of the large assembly and hovered between the Israelites and the Egyptians all night so that the Egyptians could not touch the Israelites.

Today, we're under attack. The devil seeks to destroy us, modern culture seeks to seduce us, and our own sin nature deceives us. Only the presence of God can keep us from succumbing to fear and, more ominously, falling into the sin that seeks to entangle us.

Only God can protect us and our children from the wiles of the devil. That's why Jesus prayed that we might be kept "from the evil one" (John 17:15).

Let us pray that His presence might put a barrier between us and the enemies of our souls.

A Prayer to Begin Your Time of Intercession

Father, I pray that You will protect me from the evil one. I pray that You will be a shield about me, behind, beneath, and above. Help me to detect Satan's wiles, his deceitful ways, and his suggestions. I confess my sins and receive Your forgiveness that I might be clean before You. May there be no evil crevice within my soul that gives Satan permission to tempt or harass me. Put a cloud of glory between me and Satan.

I pray for _____, that they might be protected from Satan's designs. Put distance between them and sin; place Your Spirit between them and the deceptions of the flesh. Protect them from lies that permeate our culture, from pornography, from sexual temptations. Protect them from evil people, from those who would deceive, manipulate, or even destroy. Deliver us from all evil, I pray. I trust Your Word to do as You have promised.

In Jesus' name, Amen.

A Prayer for the Fear of the Lord

"Now when all the people saw the thunder and the flashes of lightning and the sound of the trumpet and the mountain smoking, the people were afraid and trembled, and they stood far off and said to Moses, 'You speak to us, and we will listen; but do not let God speak to us, lest we die.' Moses said to the people, 'Do not fear, for God has come to test you, that the fear of him may be before you, that you may not sin.'"

—Exodus 20:18-20

Is it true that the fear of God is simply an Old Testament concept that disappeared with the coming of Christ? Is it safer to sin under grace than it was under law?

The decisive answer is no. The fear of the Lord is also repeatedly mentioned and commanded in the New Testament. For example, in the book of Acts we read that the early church "going on in the fear of the Lord...continued to increase" (9:31 NASB). Peter said that we should live our lives before God with "reverent fear" (1 Peter 1:17 NIV).

God's holiness demands our respect and fear. And, yes, that fear includes being afraid of God.

When God appeared on Mount Sinai, the people were terrified, so Moses made this interesting statement: "Do not fear, for God has come to test you, that the fear of him may be before you, that you may not sin" (Exodus 20:20).

Follow this carefully: On the one hand, the people were not to tremble in fear. Yet on the other hand, God had come to reveal Himself so that they *would* fear Him and keep His commandments. So the people were told *not* to fear God; but at the same time they *were* to fear Him as a deterrent to sin.

How do we explain this apparent contradiction?

I agree with one writer who points out that God was, in effect, saying that the Israelites should not fear God as slaves fear their masters. Rather, they were to fear Him as sons. The fear of a slave causes him to cower; he looks to his master with trepidation. But "son fear" is something different—it motivates us to seek and please God.

Think of it this way: Moses, who feared God as a son fears his father, went straight up the mountain to pursue God more intensely. His fear of the Lord motivated him to holiness, as was also true of the apostle Paul (2 Corinthians 7:1). Jesus Himself took delight in the fear of the Lord (Isaiah 11:2-3). "Slave fear" that drives us away from God is wrong; "son fear" that drives us toward God is right and proper.

We should fear God because we know that our sin displeases Him. If we love God, we will not want to incur His displeasure. And when we offend Him by grieving the Holy Spirit, we should fear that our love of sin is greater than our love of God.

The path to destruction begins when we no longer fear God—for then we will not fear sin, but we'll think that we can control the consequences. Many a life has been wrecked on such deceptions.

Let us pray that we might fear the Lord as His sons and daughters. Let us ask Him to give us a vision of His holiness and justice that makes us "tremble at his word" as the prophet Isaiah admonishes us to do (Isaiah 66:5). Let us pray that we might "serve the LORD with fear, and rejoice with trembling" (Psalm 2:11).

A Prayer to Begin Your Time of Intercession

Father, I pray that You might enable me to have such a grand vision of You that I might fear You, that I might tremble in Your presence. Help me to see that You're not merely a Redeemer but also a Judge; not merely a God of love, but also of holiness. Help me to fear sin not just because of its consequences, but also because it grieves Your heart. As your child, I pray that I might "serve the LORD with fear, and rejoice with trembling" as we're admonished to do.

What I pray for myself, I also pray for _____ and ask that they might fear You just as a son or daughter fears a Father who both loves and disciplines—a Father who extends mercy but also judges.

Above all, may they fear You because they love You and seek to please You through Jesus Christ. May the fear of the Lord keep them from sin, and in turn, may the grace of the Lord keep them walking in obedience.

In Jesus' name, Amen.

A Prayer for Holiness

*"Speak to all the congregation of the people of Israel and say to
them, 'You shall be holy, for I the LORD your God am holy.'"*
—LEVITICUS 19:2

There are many ways in which we cannot be like God; we'll never possess attributes such as omniscience, omnipotence, or omnipresence. But one way in which we can, in a measure, be like Him, is in the matter of holiness. "You shall be holy, for I...am holy" is a scriptural refrain.

In a word, we are to be imitators of God in matters of holiness. A holy life should be the goal of each of us as His children.

Holiness, when applied to God, means that He is "separate" from His creation; He is "wholly other," unlike anything or anyone that you and I know. When applied to us, it means that we are "separated unto God." That means we are separated from worldly values and entertainment; we are increasingly intolerant of sin and increasingly more dependent on Christ, who represents us to the Father and meets God's ultimate standard of holiness on our behalf.

So while on the one hand Jesus is our holiness, we are also to strive in faith to pursue holiness. To put it differently, our holiness is objective (found in Christ), but also subjective (to be lived out in our daily lives). Our part is to pursue the disciplines of the Christian life: daily Scripture reading, prayer, accountability to other believers, private and corporate worship, and in general, vigilance, and of course, both submission and faith.

Jesus said that Satan had no claim on Him (John 14:30). To be holy means that there is no part of us that is held back from God's control. Holiness means that I'm seeking God to help me to be separate from sin and totally separated to Him and His will. Such holiness is not optional; *the Scriptures teach that we are saved in order to become holy!*

Let us pray that we will be free from unconquered sin. Let us affirm that Christ is our holiness—and as we look to Him, let us also desire to be as holy as is possible for sinners to be! Let us pray that we will love righteousness (holiness) and hate iniquity.

A Prayer to Begin Your Time of Intercession

Father, I pray that I might love holiness; show me the deceitfulness of sin that I might turn from it. I rejoice that Jesus is my holiness. Help me to draw from Him all that I need to follow Him in His love of righteousness. Give me a desire to turn from my sin by pursuing the disciplines of the Christian life that keep me connected with You all day long.

And Lord, I pray for _____, that they might realize that at first, sin always appears harmless; that they might realize that a single seed can bring a destructive harvest. Therefore, I pray that they might, first of all, look to Christ as their holiness. Then that they would, in obedience, pursue the disciplines of the Christian life, such as Your Word that washes our minds; Your presence that directs our hearts; and Your Son who is our Advocate who stands ready to forgive us.

I pray that we might not settle for living a defeated life. I pray that the intercession of Christ might assure us that an increasing degree of holiness is possible thanks to His grace and power. Give us a love for God that is always accompanied by a love of holiness.

In Jesus' name, Amen.

A Prayer for God's Favor

"The LORD spoke to Moses, saying, 'Speak to Aaron and his sons, saying, Thus you shall bless the people of Israel: you shall say to them, "The LORD bless you and keep you; The LORD make his face to shine upon you and be gracious to you; The LORD lift up his countenance upon you and give you peace." So shall they put my name upon the people of Israel, and I will bless them.'"

—NUMBERS 6:22-27

What a difference "face time" makes! Today in business, networking by using Skype is preferable to connecting by telephone because you can see each other. Facebook has transformed social media because people want to connect with their friends more directly. Emails are helpful but impersonal; Facebook is more direct; but Skype enables the parties to connect with direct facial representation. Of course, even the best form of social media is no substitute for direct face-to-face time in the presence of one another.

Just so, we should all desire "face time" with God. Daniel Henderson writes, "The idea of God's face is one of the most powerful, life-changing themes of the Bible."[1] And indeed it is. When we study the word *face* as used in Scripture, we see it means "the representation of the real essence or character of a person." No wonder we're encouraged to seek God's face as Moses did on Mount Sinai. And, because face-to-face encounters are the most intimate, every believer anticipates the day when we shall see Jesus face-to-face.

Sin causes us to hide our faces from God (as Adam and Eve did); and we read that God is spoken of as hiding His face from His people when they refused to turn away from their sin in order to pursue Him (for example, Psalm 13:1). We have the same teaching in the New Testament: "For the eyes of the Lord are on the righteous, and his ears are open to their prayer. But the face of the Lord is against those who do evil" (1 Peter 3:12).

God asked Moses to pray that His people might be blessed with the highest honor—namely, to have His face "shine upon" them. With this, they could endure adversity; they could resist temptation; and they would not fear, for they would be enjoying the very face (presence) of God.

Today, we're invited to seek God's face. "Seek the LORD and His strength; seek His face continually!" (1 Chronicles 16:11 NASB). Let us respond, "When you said, 'Seek My face' my heart said to You, 'Your face, LORD, I will seek'" (Psalm 27:8). So let us seek His face, and in this way "put His name" on ourselves and others, just as Moses was invited to do.

A Prayer to Begin Your Time of Intercession

Father, I come to You without a prayer list. I come simply to seek Your face, to seek intimacy with You, to be in Your presence, and to enjoy Your company. Reveal any sin in my life that interferes with face-to-face fellowship. Grant me the grace to be open with You, hiding nothing and being enveloped by Your grace and love.

I pray for _____, that they might seek Your face and not just Your hand. Reveal to them the importance of coming before You in openness and honesty, desiring to have fellowship with You, and rejoicing in Your favor. Give them the deep conviction that seeking You is their first and highest priority, the source of all blessing and the very reason for their existence.

Help them to confess the sins that stand in the way of open communion in Your blessed presence. In this way I "put Your name on _____."

In Jesus' name, Amen.

A Prayer That We Not Be Ashamed of the Gospel

"I am not ashamed of the gospel, for it is the power of God for salvation to everyone who believes, to the Jew first and also to the Greek. For in it the righteousness of God is revealed from faith for faith, as it is written, 'The righteous shall live by faith.'"

—ROMANS 1:16-17

Why would anyone be ashamed of the gospel? Why does Paul pray that he might not be ashamed of this message of hope and salvation? The answer is that the gospel is offensive to the unconverted person. The very notion that the death of a man on a cross 2000 years ago is the only basis for our entry into heaven is so contrary to our natural instincts that, at first blush, the unsaved are inclined to reject it as absurd.

First, it's difficult for the natural man to even accept the idea that God is angry with sinners, and therefore, needs a sacrifice in order to be appeased. Our culture tells us that God is relatively happy with us, and if He isn't, He should get over being so narrow and judgmental.

Second, the fact that Jesus was God and yet allowed Himself to be shamefully crucified is a stretch for unbelievers to accept. If He is the King of kings and Lord of lords, why wouldn't He vanquish His enemies by the breath of His mouth? The Greeks thought—and many today agree—that any god who is humiliated must, by definition, be very weak and therefore unworthy of worship.

And finally, the very idea that we cannot save ourselves by our good deeds and our attempts at doing the best we can is a blow to our pride. We think that as long as we are able to live with our conscience, God should be able to live with us and be happy with our attempts to be good. Like one man said, "If God doesn't accept me, He should lighten up!"

This explains why we must pray that we will not be ashamed of the gospel. It is indeed the power of God unto salvation, but we are tempted to "hide it under a bushel"—to be silent about our faith and to be embarrassed about what we believe. Imagine—Jesus is not ashamed of us, and yet, often His followers are ashamed of Him!

We need to be freed from our fear of witnessing, freed from the hesitation we might have of sharing the one message that can bring a sinner to God. It's indeed a sad commentary on human nature that the message which the world regards as foolish is actually the only message that can redeem it!

A Prayer to Begin Your Time of Intercession

Father, forgive us for being ashamed of the gospel; forgive us for those times when we have not shared the very truth that has saved us. We repent of all fear of witnessing to our faith in the Lord Jesus Christ.

I pray for _____, that they might be so committed to Jesus that they might never be ashamed of Him. Help them to gladly identify with Him, both in His sufferings and in His victories. May we never be intimidated by our peers. Please deliver us from those habitual sins that condemn our conscience and make us feel so unworthy of telling others of Jesus' grace and power. May we be such lovers of the gospel that we are eager to share it both in word and deed.

In Jesus' name, Amen.

A Prayer for Assurance

"All who are led by the Spirit of God are sons of God. For you
did not receive the spirit of slavery to fall back into fear, but you
have received the Spirit of adoption as sons, by whom we cry,
'Abba! Father!' The Spirit himself bears witness with our spirit
that we are children of God, and if children, then heirs—heirs
of God and fellow heirs with Christ, provided we suffer with
him in order that we may also be glorified with him."

—ROMANS 8:14-17

God has given us many benefits through faith in Christ. Among them is the gift of the Holy Spirit, who leads us, even though at times we may be unaware of it. He also ministers to our human spirit, giving us the assurance that we belong to God.

Paul says that we who belong to God are led by the Spirit in our struggle against sin, but the Spirit also gives us the gift of the assurance. He says the Spirit enables us to cry, "Abba! Father!" That word "Abba" is Aramaic for "daddy"—the word a child would use for his father. Yes, it's the Spirit who inspires and enables us to call God "Father," thus affirming that we are His sons and daughters.

In Islam, it is anathema to call God "Father." But, in contrast, Paul taught that "Abba! Father!" is the witness the Holy Spirit gives us that assures us that we are God's children. This assurance entails an invitation to come into His blessed presence. The Spirit of God gives that sense of certainty only to believers in Christ.

At a recent Chicago Marathon, I noticed the words "For My Father" imprinted on a runner's T-shirt, along with an arrow pointing upward. Very likely, this man was running for his dad, who had died, and now the runner was hoping that his father was watching from above. When I saw the words, I thought of all the training that this man must have gone through and the hardship he endured in preparing for this grueling race. He was running the race for his earthly father; how much more eager we should be to run the race for our heavenly Father!

The Son died for us, the Holy Spirit leads us, and the Father adopts us. We are given the "Spirit of adoption." A baby who inherits a million dollars cannot enjoy it because he or she has to be an adult to enter into the inheritance. But Paul taught that God adopts us immediately when we receive Christ as Savior so that we can begin to enjoy our inheritance here on earth.

And finally, someday in heaven, the Son will crown us. We are, after all, heirs of God and fellow heirs with Jesus Christ. An heir of God receives all that God has, and he inherits God Himself. And to think the Word and the Spirit bear witness that all of this will be ours!

Let us pray for the gift of assurance.

A Prayer to Begin Your Time of Intercession

Father, I pray that You might give me such a peaceful sense of assurance that I might never doubt that You own me; I am Yours both now and forever. I pray that I might let the promises of Your Word guide me during the dark times; I pray that my faith might grow each day in my walk with You.

I pray for _____, that they might treasure Your promises. Let Your Word be internalized within them; cause Your truth to be their strength and joy. Deliver them from any false assurance based on a "decision" that might not have resulted in saving faith. Deliver them from the presumption that they are one of your children if they have based their belief on a false understanding of salvation.

Where there is true faith, may it grow with such certainty that we become as confident of heaven as though we are already there. Thank You for the Spirit who cries within us, "Abba! Father!"

In Jesus' name, Amen.

Week 16

A Prayer for Faithfulness in Suffering

"I consider that the sufferings of this present time are not worth
comparing with the glory that is to be revealed to us...
but we ourselves, who have the firstfruits of the Spirit, groan
inwardly as we wait eagerly for adoption as sons,
the redemption of our bodies."

—ROMANS 8:18,23

Our suffering is often a challenge to our faith. In fact, most of us aren't good at suffering. After all, we think if God loved us, He would remove the obstacles that bring us so much anguish and pain.

Faith healers are right to believe that Jesus died on the cross for us body, soul, and spirit, and that redemption is total. But they fail to point out that we do not receive all the benefits of Jesus' death until we die and our souls go to heaven. Then later we will be resurrected, and the promise of our full redemption will be realized.

Don't ever minimize the value of suffering. In Scripture, we are called to maintain our faith in God's promises during our times of suffering. *Tested faith is of great value to God.*

The apostle Paul wrote, "[This] light affliction, which is but for a moment, is working for us a far more exceeding and eternal weight of glory" (2 Corinthians 4:17 NKJV). Put all your suffering on one side of the scale, and the glory that is to be revealed in us on the other side, and the scale will fall over from the weight of the glory to come. God will make up for our suffering many times over. Our current afflictions are unworthy of comparison.

The glory that will be revealed in us can only be partially imagined. It's not just that we'll have glorified bodies; we will also "appear with Jesus in glory," joined by our believing loved ones. So in the end, everything we will have endured on this earth will be worth it all. Our past sorrows will disappear, and we will live in glory forevermore.

Until that day when we see Jesus, Paul says, we will groan inwardly for the redemption of our bodies—and it is for our future glory that we groan.

A Prayer to Begin Your Time of Intercession

Father, help us to suffer well. Let us learn from your Son, "the Man of sorrows," how to maintain our faith even in the face of affliction. Let us never turn away from You no matter how dark the night and fearful the future. Teach us to go on believing Your promises even without explanations.

I pray for _____, that they might be steadfast when suffering comes their way. Let them be assured that no matter the temperature within the furnace of affliction, You keep Your hand on the thermostat. Help us to know You well enough to trust You and be faithful until we see You face-to-face.

In Jesus' name, Amen.

Prayer is a sincere, sensible, affectionate
pouring out of the soul to God, through Christ,
in the strength and assistance of the Spirit,
for such things as God has promised.

John Bunyan

A Prayer for Freedom from Self-Incrimination

"Who shall bring any charge against God's elect? It is God who justifies. Who is to condemn? Christ Jesus is the one who died— more than that, who was raised—who is at the right hand of God, who indeed is interceding for us."

—ROMANS 8:33-34

There are millions of people who go to church on Sunday and confess their sins, but they are not converted as a result of this exercise. If we had to confess all our sins in order to be saved, salvation would be beyond reach. For one thing, we can't remember all our sins, and even if we could, tomorrow is another day with new sins. It would be like wiping the floor with the faucet running!

When God saves us, He has to absolve us from *all* our sins—past, present, and future—in one divine act. He does this by crediting us with the righteousness of Jesus Christ in response to saving faith. By that act, we are legally perfect forever.

Twenty-four hours a day, God demands that we be perfect if He is to fellowship with us and welcome us into heaven at death; twenty-four hours a day, Jesus Christ supplies what God demands. Jesus stands in for us on our behalf, and we are accepted as if we were Him.

Yes, of course we as Christians confess our sins on an ongoing basis to maintain fellowship with God. But our legal standing before God remains unchanged despite our continuing struggles with sin and failure. The unchangeable righteousness of Christ, once credited to us, is never diminished nor removed from us.

So who *can* bring a charge against God's elect? Your conscience can. Other people can. And of course, there's the devil, who accuses the saints day and night. In response, Paul says, "It is God who justi-fies." And, what is more, Jesus, even now, intercedes for us. Only such assurance silences our conscience—our judge within.

Personally, I rely upon this truth every day: I remind myself that my heavenly Father sees me as being "in Christ," and thereby my guilt is removed and my conscience is stilled. We must pray that we and other believers will depend upon this blessed reality whenever we are overcome by regret and guilt.

A Prayer to Begin Your Time of Intercession

Father, open my eyes to the reality that Christ's righteousness is mine. May I, despite my struggles with sin, rejoice that Jesus represents me to You. Though I mourn over my sins, may I not be disheartened. Help me to look to Jesus, and not my own performance, as a basis of my acceptance.

I pray for _____, that they might be satisfied with what Jesus has done on their behalf. May they be freed from the condemnation of sin, and rest in the assurance that they've been accepted in the Beloved One. Each morning, let them rise to renew their confidence in the promise that Jesus has made them pleasing to You. May the discour-agement that so often leads to a downward spiral of sin vanish when they remember that no one can bring a charge against God's elect with-out being met by the declaration that they have been forever justified.

In Jesus' name, Amen.

A Prayer to Rest Confidently in the Love of God

"Who shall separate us from the love of Christ? Shall tribulation, or distress, or persecution, or famine, or nakedness, or danger, or sword?...No, in all these things we are more than conquerors through him who loved us. For I am sure that neither death nor life, nor angels nor rulers, nor things present nor things to come, nor powers, nor height nor depth, nor anything else in all creation, will be able to separate us from the love of God in Christ Jesus our Lord."

—ROMANS 8:35,37-39

Author Larry Crabb said that a friend of his wrote these words to him: "When God does so little about things that matter so much to me, I have no categories for understanding God's statement that He loves me. I'm grateful that my sins are forgiven and I'm going to heaven, and I know that all of these troubles are somehow useful for good purposes, maybe necessary for making me a more godly person, but I can't get past the thought that real love wouldn't let me suffer like this."[2]

After listing nine different tragedies that can befall us—such as tribulation, persecution, famine, and sword (being martyred)—Paul affirms that none of these events, nor any other created thing, can separate us from the love of Christ. In fact, we are "more than conquerors through him who loved us."

But how do we conquer in the midst of difficult circumstances when there's little outward evidence that God loves us? Jerry Bridges has observed that "God's unfailing love for us is an objective fact affirmed over and over in the Scriptures. It is true whether we believe it or not."[3] So no matter what our external circumstances, we can fully trust God's love for us based on the many promises of His love as stated in the Bible.

Anyone who continues to trust God no matter what could possibly happen to him is a super-conqueror. God is glorified when we place complete trust in Him regardless of our circumstances. His love not only endures, it triumphs. Life, with all of its difficulties and dangers, cannot separate us from Christ's love, nor can angels or principalities (rulers in the demonic world). These evil rulers can harass, confuse, and even win victories over Christians, but they can't separate us from the love of Christ. The events of today, and the things you will face tomorrow, cannot separate you from the love of Christ.

Divine love is based on the lover, not on the one who is loved. Of course the best evidence that God loves us is seen at the cross: "This is love, not that we have loved God but that he loved us and sent his Son to be the propitiation for our sins" (1 John 4:10). God will never be dissuaded from loving those whom He has chosen to redeem.

Charles Spurgeon said, "Oh blessed axe of sorrow that cuts a pathway to my God by chopping down the tall trees of human comfort."[4] Sorrow doesn't separate us from God's love. Instead, it should drive us toward Him. So the frightened believer who is pressed by circumstances can still hope in God; God has taken him through a difficult patch, but he is not separated from His love.

In 1842, George Matheson, though blind, went to the University of Glasgow (his sister read his textbooks to him) and became a pastor. He memorized his sermons and the Scriptures every Sunday so that he knew the Word. But at one point he went through a time of depression and doubted God's love, and even left the ministry. He eventually came back with a renewed vigor and faith, and later wrote:

> O Love that wilt not let me go,
> I rest my weary soul in thee;
> I give thee back the life I owe,
> That in Thine ocean depths its flow may richer, fuller be.[5]

A Prayer to Begin Your Time of Intercession

Father, help us cleave to Your promises that we might know we are loved. We thank You for those "providences" we see in our lives that remind us of Your care and Your grace. Yet may we remember that the proof of Your love for us doesn't exist in our circumstances or answered prayers, but that it's seen most clearly at the cross.

I pray for _____, that they might not doubt Your love. I pray that they will be strengthened by the assurances of Your care that comes from Your Word. Cause Your love to motivate them to obedience, surrender, and joyous worship. Today, may we all rejoice in the sure knowledge that we are loved.

In Jesus' name, Amen.

A Prayer for Greater Love for God

"You shall love the LORD your God with all your heart and with all your soul and with all your might."
—DEUTERONOMY 6:5

Love is not an emotion that can be turned on or off like a faucet. Love—true love—involves a deep and abiding commitment to the one who is loved. Of course it involves the emotions, but it is also rooted in the mind and the will. We show this kind of love when we are willing to surrender our lives for the good of someone else. In fact, in Deuteronomy 6:5, as in so many other places in the Bible, we are exhorted to love from our heart, a reference to the very core of our being.

If we loved God with all our heart, soul, and might, it would affect every aspect of our lives—how we treat others, how we view our vocation, how we earn and spend money, and how much time we spend in God's presence. We would become, in the best sense of the word, "God-intoxicated." Such a love for God is actually the major, and ultimately, the only purpose of our existence. And such love gives us a distaste for sin.

But how do we love God when, by nature, we're prone to turn away from Him? How do we learn to love a God whose wrath abides on all those who reject His Son?

First, we must meditate on Him through the lens of Scripture. We can't say we're in a love relationship with Him and spend scant time in the letter He sent us via the authors of the Bible. We must ask God to show Himself to us through His Word, and we cannot know Him well unless we make an effort to know His Word well.

Second, unconfessed sin drains our love for God out of our hearts.

When we engage in the sensuality of worldly pleasures and live with a troubled or unclean conscience, we will be robbed of our freedom and joy in God's presence. A thorough confession of and turning away from sin will restore the fellowship and love that we are meant to enjoy as His children.

Finally, we must contemplate the cross and try to grasp how far God reached in order to save us. We must realize His great love toward us. "We love because he first loved us" (1 John 4:19). The more we minimize the seriousness of our sin, the more we will minimize the cross; and the more we minimize the cross, the less appreciation we have for God. The first commandment is to love Him, but we can't obey that command without divine intervention and help.

A Prayer to Begin Your Time of Intercession

Father, cleanse our lives from the clutter that dampens our love for You. We confess the false loves that have become a cheap substitute for loving You. Show us, Lord, what stands in the way of obeying You and loving You with all our being. May our love for You be constant, pure, and focused.

I pray for_____. I ask that You will show them Your beauty so that that they might see that You're deserving of our adoration, our worship, and the love of our hearts. Father, _____ is weak, and like the rest of us, prone to love the world—to love self more than to love You. Father, create within them a love for You that is greater than their love of sin. Cause them to remember that You loved us first— that despite our sin, Your favor, given to us in Jesus Christ, leads us to love You with our whole heart. Let that love be kept fresh through Your Word and through worship.

In Jesus' name, Amen.

A Prayer for Your Family and Our National Leaders

"These words that I command you today shall be on your heart.
You shall teach them diligently to your children, and shall talk
of them when you sit in your house, and when you walk by the
way, and when you lie down, and when you rise."
—DEUTERONOMY 6:6-7

"Behold, I will send you Elijah the prophet before the great
and awesome day of the LORD comes. And he will turn
the hearts of fathers to their children and the hearts of
children to their fathers, lest I come and strike the land with
a decree of utter destruction."
—MALACHI 4:5-6

Take a moment and respond to this challenge: What is the first word that comes to your mind when you see the word *father*?

Was the descriptive word you used positive or negative? Perhaps you answered "dedicated," or "preoccupied," or "harsh," or even "abusive." Or perhaps you never knew your father, so you said, "Absent." At any rate, how you answer that question reveals much about you. Even if you never met your father, he still has power over you; his influence in your life continues for good or for ill.

Mike Singletary, former linebacker for the Chicago Bears, often speaks in prisons and asks this question of the inmates: How many of you can say you had a warm relationship with your father? In an article I read, he said he is still waiting for the first hand to be raised! With millions of children in America going to bed each night without a father in the home, we can only imagine what the consequences will be—both now and in future generations.

In the Scripture passages above, God clearly holds the father responsible for being both the lawgiver and the grace-giver in the home. He is to teach the children and model for them what walking with God looks like. And as the verses from Malachi indicate, there is to be mutual reconciliation and fellowship between a father and his family. The heart of the father should be turned toward his children, and the hearts of the children to their father. If not, there are drastic consequences.

The prayer we will pray for this week is one that intercedes for those fathers who are good examples for their children, as well as those fathers who have neglected their families—who are abusive, harsh, and uncaring. We will also pray for those children who either don't know their father, or who have a lingering bitterness because of their father's misdeeds.

Even if your father is no longer living, I encourage you to pray this week's prayer. You can either pray for a father you know, or more generally, for a dysfunctional family. Or you can pray for your own family. Feel free to adapt the prayer for whatever God may lay upon your heart.

A Prayer to Begin Your Time of Intercession

Father, I want to thank You for my father. Whether he lived up to my expectations or not, he was chosen to give me physical life, and I was chosen to be born at a place and time designated by You. Thank You for my parents, for their strengths and their weaknesses.

And now, Father, I pray for the children who are struggling because of their relationship with their father. I pray for _____, that they might be reconciled to their father. Take away the bitterness and the anger that exists in that home, and bring peace to the family. And as for _____, who either has failed or is failing as a father, bring him to his senses that he might become Your servant and see his need to become the role model You intended. Break the power of addictions, hate, and rejection that have deeply wounded this family. Help fathers to confess their failures to their children, and children confess their failures to their fathers. At all costs, bring them into a right relationship with You and with each other.

In Jesus' name, Amen.

A Prayer to Meditate on the Scriptures

"This Book of the Law shall not depart from your mouth, but you shall meditate on it day and night, so that you may be careful to do according to all that is written in it. For then you will make your way prosperous, and then you will have good success."

—Joshua 1:8

Most of us wish that God would work on us while we're asleep so that we could wake to face the day with unwavering confidence and faith! We wish that good intentions, combined with attending church once a week, would bring about permanent changes in our attitudes and behavior. How nice it would be if our spiritual laziness was offset by our good intentions. Then we could sit back, relax, and still become spiritual giants!

The simple fact is that we are not going to live differently until we think differently; and we will not think differently unless we have the discipline to learn to think God's thoughts after Him. Paul wrote that we should not be conformed to this world, "but be transformed by the renewal of your mind" (Romans 12:2). It is quite correct to say, "You are not what you think you are...but *what you think, you are.*"

Only meditation in the Scriptures can change our thinking. But how do we learn to meditate?

We begin by praying, "Open my eyes, that I may behold wondrous things out of your law" (Psalm 119:18). Somewhere I read, "As long as my mind is raging with thoughts, ideas, plans, and fears, I cannot listen significantly to God or any other dimension of reality." How true!

Before we go through the following steps, open your Bible right now to a passage of Scripture—perhaps somewhere in the book of Psalms—and begin the process of meditation.

Step one: *Analyze*. Ask these questions about the text: What does this passage teach me about God? Is there a promise to be believed? Is there a step of obedience I need to take?

Step two: *Personalize*. Choose to bring your life under the authority of God's Word. Ask: What difference should this passage make to me? What sin am I aware of that I must confess? What truth or verse can I take with me today? Don't close your Bible until your heart is at peace and you have either a verse or a phrase that you can take with you for the rest of the day. Ask God to give you something to chew on!

Step three: *Memorize*. My experience has been that when I memorize Scripture, my mind is purified and continually being refocused on the Lord and His promises. Even memorizing a snatch of Scripture enables us to hide God's Word in our hearts as a protection against temptation and stray thoughts that rob us of our faith and joy.

I like the story about an American tourist who bought a special jewelry box in France with the assurance that it would glow in the dark. He took it home and put it on his dresser, but it didn't live up to the promise he was given. A friend who was able to read French looked at the instructions, which said, "Put me in the sunshine during the day, and then I will glow in the dark."

Do you want to glow in the dark, spiritually speaking? You must meditate in the law of God, and you will see transformation. And yes, you will "glow in the dark."

A Prayer to Begin Your Time of Intercession

Father, give me the discipline to meditate in Your Word "day and night." Teach me to hide Your Word in my heart that I might not sin against You. Help me to have the discipline to do this, and may I be motivated by my loving relationship with You.

I pray for _____, who is struggling spiritually, neglecting Your Word, perhaps deliberately, perhaps because he finds Your Word confusing or irrelevant. Help them to come back to Your promises, back to reading Your Book, and taking the time to think about it, analyze it, personalize it, and even memorize it. Lord, give them a desire to live by every word that proceeds out of Your mouth.

I pray in Jesus' name, Amen.

A Prayer to Put Away Sinful Practices

"Now therefore fear the LORD and serve him in sincerity and in faithfulness. Put away the gods that your fathers served beyond the River and in Egypt, and serve the LORD. And if it is evil in your eyes to serve the LORD, choose this day whom you will serve, whether the gods your fathers served in the region beyond the River, or the gods of the Amorites in whose land you dwell. But as for me and my house, we will serve the LORD."

—JOSHUA 24:14-15

If we think of idolatry as referring only to worshipping pagan gods, we've missed an important bit of truth in our own walk with God. Ezekiel wrote that the people of Israel were "taking their idols into their hearts" (see Ezekiel 14:4). Idolatry is a matter of mental images that we cling to, whether the aspirations of the flesh, or preoccupation with our own selfish ambition. To put it clearly, idolatry is nothing more than valuing something else more than we do God and our relationship to Him.

Joshua asked that the people of Israel put their idols behind them. In their case, that meant smashing the physical idols that they had brought with them out of Egypt. We should not be surprised that the people had brought their "gods" with them from Egypt, for false deities are actually empowered by demonic forces, and for this reason it's difficult to break these occult attachments. Witness, for example, the difficulty some people in Japan have had in breaking away from the tradition of worshipping their ancestors, or a Catholic's inordinate preoccupation with a crucifix. Humans find it difficult to break attachments to physical objects, but mental idolatry is just as captivating and addictive.

This week we will pray about smashing our idols, specifically habitual sins or addictions that hold us captive to our own lusts and desires. Whether it is possessions, personal pursuits, achievements, sexual addictions, or alcohol or drugs, these kinds of obsessions and sins and others like them have great power over the human will. Human determination, though laudable, simply cannot break these bondages.

Here are a few lines I memorized some time ago from William Cowper's hymn "O for a Closer Walk with God":

> The dearest idol I have known,
> Whate'er that idol be
> Help me to tear it from Thy throne,
> And worship only Thee.[6]

The following is a spiritual warfare prayer that seeks to enlist God's help and strength in the deepest crevices of the soul.

A Prayer to Begin Your Time of Intercession

Father, all of us are prone to idolatry; indeed, our minds are constantly manufacturing new idols. We are so prone to wander from You. Today we confess our sins; show us our idols, but also show us how destructive they are and how they grieve Your Spirit. We pray that we might "put away" our idols so that we might not repeat the same sins. Break the power of Satan on our behalf.

And now I pray for _____. I pray that You will reveal their idols to them; show them Your hatred for sin, but also show them Your amazing grace. Like the rest of us, _____ is too weak to overthrow the idols of the heart. We are all bound by the cords of sin, trying to manage it rather than breaking free of it.

Lord, we are desperate for Your deliverance. Show us what we must do to put away our idols, and then grant us the grace to do it. Like Israel of old, let us take the idols we've hidden, expose them, and then throw them at Your feet to be smashed forever. We trust Your Spirit to do this in us for Your glory.

In Jesus' name, Amen.

A Prayer for Unsaved Friends

*"I am speaking the truth in Christ—I am not lying; my
conscience bears me witness in the Holy Spirit—that I have
great sorrow and unceasing anguish in my heart. For I could
wish that I myself were accursed and cut off from Christ for the
sake of my brothers, my kinsmen according to the flesh."*

—ROMANS 9:1-3

*"Brothers, my heart's desire and prayer to God for them [Israel]
is that they may be saved. For I bear them witness that they have
a zeal for God, but not according to knowledge."*

—ROMANS 10:1-2

We are well acquainted with Paul's heart for believers—the church of Jesus Christ. But in these passages we see his tender burden for the unsaved, especially for Jews who continued in their devotion to the law rather than trusting the finished work of Jesus Christ. No matter how much concern we have for an unsaved friend or child, it is doubtful that we would have a burden so heavy that we would be willing to go to hell in the place of that person! Imagine Paul's heart.

We should note that these words were written by the same man who also taught the doctrine of election—that is, that salvation is ultimately in the hands of God, not the hands of men. In the very same chapter where Paul wrote that we are clay in the hands of the potter, and that God "has mercy on whomever he wills, and he hardens whomever he wills" (Romans 9:18), he also spoke about his great burden for his Jewish brothers according to the flesh (see 9:1-3 above). The bottom line: *The sovereign election of God does not nullify the fact that we should be contending for the souls of unbelievers.*

We should be praying for the unsaved, pleading with God on their behalf. The unconverted are dead in trespasses and sins; they are blind to the gospel, and they are deaf to the truth of God's Word. Who can overcome their darkness and grant them the gift of salvation? Who can create a new nature within them and set them free from their own blindness and self-absorption? Only God can intervene and save them.

And who can rid us of our selfishness so that believers have a burden for their unsaved friends and relatives? Who can birth within us a passionate concern for the eternal destiny of the lost? Who but the Spirit can motivate us to pray earnestly that they might be saved?

The following prayer is not just for the unsaved. It's also for us, that we might share Paul's burden for the lost. We must confess our own complacency and invite God to grant us the passion to experience the joy of the Father's forgiveness and the warmth of the Father's love. We must pray for ourselves before we pray for the lost.

Let us open our hearts now and invite the Spirit to give us Paul's heart for others, and then contend for the souls of those who need the Savior.

A Prayer to Begin Your Time of Intercession

Father, forgive me for my selfish disregard for my friends and neighbors who are lost in their sins and trespasses. I pray that You might break my heart for the lost, and that I might give myself to earnest intercession for their salvation. And help me to present a loving witness to them as I have opportunity. Give me the passion of Paul for a world that has lost its way.

And now I pray for _____, that they might be drawn to Jesus Christ for salvation. I pray that You, O Lord, might cause them to see their sins, and that they might cry to You and be saved. Lord, make them discontent with their self-help solutions and their misguided quests for personal peace and significance. Show them the glories of Jesus, not just as Savior, but as Lord and King. Cause them to believe on Him and be saved.

In Jesus' name, Amen.

A Prayer to Worship God More Fervently

"Oh, the depth of the riches and wisdom and knowledge of God! How unsearchable are his judgments and how inscrutable his ways! For who has known the mind of the Lord, or who has been his counselor? Or who has given a gift to him that he might be repaid? For from him and through him and to him are all things. To him be glory forever. Amen."

—ROMANS 11:33-36

Paul rejoices in God's sovereignty in Israel's history, both in the nation's past blindness and eventual future eagerness to embrace Jesus as Messiah. Contemplating the mysterious and yet glorious greatness of God and His purposes, Paul breaks out with adoration and humble worship. Surely we all agree that at this point we enter a realm that is beyond our experience.

The word "unsearchable" means "untraceable," which stresses that our knowledge of God is limited. Theologians are right to tell us that we can know God truly, but of course we cannot know Him exhaustively. "Your way was through the sea, your path through the great waters; yet your footprints were unseen" (Psalm 77:19).

Paul asks two questions in Romans 11:34-35. First: "Who has known the mind of the Lord, or who has been his counselor?" The answer, of course, is that God does not need consultants; He never forms a committee for input, nor does He have to spend time trying to assess the consequences of His actions. He has everything under His sovereign control and knows all things, both actual and possible.

Next, Paul asks, "Who has given a gift to him that he might be repaid?" That is, does God need our gifts? Is He lacking in something we can help with? No, for we can give Him nothing that He has not given to us in the first place. All things originate from Him, all things continue by His powerful hand, and all things contribute to His ultimate glory. God's only restrictions are those He places upon Himself.

This week let our prayers focus on the adoration and worship of our heavenly Father. Let our requests be few, and our praises be exuberant and spontaneous.

A Prayer to Begin Your Time of Intercession

Father, we pray that You might impress on our hearts Your greatness and glory. Let the thought of Your complete sovereignty over all things cause us to both fear You and also to worship You with joyous awe. Let Your power and the mystery of Your purposes not discourage us, but rather, spur us on to greater faith and devotion. In our worship, let us have a settled confidence that You do all things well.

I pray for _____, that they might not rebel against Your authority in their lives. Help them to submit and humbly confess that You are God and have the right to rule as You wish among the kingdoms of men. Cause them to realize that nothing else matters except Your glory. May they thank You that we can be Your children, both now and forever.

In Jesus' name, Amen.

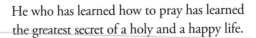

He who has learned how to pray has learned
the greatest secret of a holy and a happy life.

William Law

A Prayer That We Might Benefit from Personality Conflicts

"Let love be genuine. Abhor what is evil; hold fast to what is good.
Love one another with brotherly affection.
Outdo one another in showing honor…

"Bless those who persecute you; bless and do not curse them. Rejoice
with those who rejoice, weep with those who weep. Live in harmony
with one another. Do not be haughty, but associate with the
lowly. Never be wise in your own sight. Repay no one evil for evil,
but give thought to do what is honorable in the sight of all. If possi-
ble, so far as it depends on you, live peaceably with all. Beloved,
never avenge yourselves, but leave it to the wrath of God, for it
is written, 'Vengeance is mine, I will repay, says the Lord.' To the
contrary, 'if your enemy is hungry, feed him; if he is thirsty, give him
something to drink; for by so doing you will heap burning coals on
his head.' Do not be overcome by evil, but overcome evil with good."

—Romans 12:9-10,14-21

When confronted with difficult people, God wants us to have the characteristics of Jesus.

First, Paul says that our love should be genuine—that is, we must pray that we are not simply pretending that we love others, but that love and concern should flow from our hearts. This kind of love goes beyond human affection and springs from the love of God that "has been poured into our hearts" (Romans 5:5). As believers, we have a source of love that is unavailable to the unconverted.

Second, we should bless those who persecute us. Although these words are set in the context of the early centuries when Christians were physically persecuted in different ways, this also applies to us in our relationships with those who seek to do us harm, whether through gossip, unjust accusations, or deceitful relationships. We can bless them by praying, by asking God to bestow blessings on them, and by doing good to them. Let us do something unexpectedly good for our enemies—doing so will not only bring glory to God, but will help us to set aside any lingering bitterness we might have toward them. There is power in blessing others.

Third, we should never take vengeance into our own hands. We must trust God, for He assures us that vengeance is His responsibility. If we have faith that God will "even the score" either in this life or the life to come, we can keep entrusting the injustice done against us to God, believing that He will resolve it in His own time and in His own way. Paul ends this marvelous passage in Romans 12 by urging us to not be conquered by evil, but to conquer evil with good.

Do you have a ruptured relationship that needs resolution and healing? Do you have a child or friend who is estranged from a previous relationship? Has anger separated what at one time was a harmonious relationship? Are you daily confronted with someone who is difficult to love?

A Prayer to Begin Your Time of Intercession

Father, forgive me for being obsessed with "fairness." Help me to accept the fact that life is not fair, and to realize that the pain that I have received from relationships is intended by You to be used for Your own glory. Today, Father, fill my heart with the gift of forgiveness and the faith to believe that Your grace is able to make the best of difficult relationships. Birth within my heart the love I should have for those who have wronged me.

And I pray for _____, that they might be freed from the bitterness of a painful relationship. Help them to see that You can use a broken relationship for Your glory if it is repaired by love and forgiveness. Let their love be genuine, may they turn away from evil, and bless those who have wronged them.

In Jesus' name, Amen.

Please note: Romans 12:9-10,14-21 is so filled with practical admonitions and commands needed to create healthy relationships that I encourage you to pray the above section each day for yourself and others. When you directly pray Scripture, you put yourself in harmony with the Holy Spirit and you can be assured that you are praying God's will.

A Prayer to Be Separate from the World

"Besides this you know the time, that the hour has come for you to wake from sleep. For salvation is nearer to us now than when we first believed. The night is far gone; the day is at hand. So then let us cast off the works of darkness and put on the armor of light. Let us walk properly as in the daytime, not in orgies and drunkenness, not in sexual immorality and sensuality, not in quarreling and jealousy. But put on the Lord Jesus Christ, and make no provision for the flesh, to gratify its desires."

—ROMANS 13:11-14

In this passage, Paul gives us three commands:

First, wake up!

Have you ever been awakened from a deep sleep by an alarm or phone call? Your first reaction is to ask: What time is it? You may recall that Rip Van Winkle slept for twenty years, and when he awakened, he was surprised at all the changes that had taken place during his sleep. Here, Paul is admonishing believers to wake up, given the lateness of the hour. Spiritually speaking, we've overslept.

Unbelievers are spoken of in the Bible as being dead, but many of us who are Christians are asleep. We are totally unaware of bypassed opportunities and how close the clock is ticking down to our own death, or to the return of Christ. We need to wake up, to repent of our lack of urgency. We are also unaware of the great needs that are around us, spiritually speaking. How can we be comfortable with millions living in spiritual darkness? Like a sleepwalker who functions with little energy and no self-conscious direction, we often stumble through daily routines as if eternity didn't matter.

Next, clean up!

We are admonished, "Let us cast off the works of darkness and put on the armor of light. Let us walk properly as in the daytime" (Romans 13:12-13). The imagery of darkness represents our original spiritual state. When we walk in darkness, we stumble because stones along our path cannot be distinguished from gold, a friend cannot be distinguished from an enemy, right becomes wrong, and wrong becomes right. "The way of the wicked is like deep darkness; they do not know over what they stumble" (Proverbs 4:19).

The bottom line: Paul is saying to get rid of all those sins that are characterized by darkness, the kinds of things that you'd never want to be caught doing in the daytime. We must confess and forsake our own darkness—the hidden things that rob us of joy and power.

Finally, dress up!

Paul then wrote, "Put on the Lord Jesus Christ" (Romans 13:14). This means that we accept Christ as a Prophet—His word then becomes our bread and butter. We accept Him as our Priest for His forgiveness and intercession. We also submit to Him as King. Putting on Christ means that we clothe ourselves with all that He represents. Only such a covering can keep us from the darkness.

Paul ends this section with this exhortation: "Make no provision for the flesh, to gratify its desires" (verse 14). J.B. Phillips translates this verse, "Let us be Christ's men from head to foot, and give no chances to the flesh to have its fling."

A Prayer to Begin Your Time of Intercession

Father, forgive me for the darkness in my life—those hidden closets of the soul where sin is allowed to live and even grow. Forgive my lack of spiritual awareness, my lack of urgency for the responsibility of representing You to this world. And, Lord, I'm aware that I've often made provision for the flesh by the television I've watched and the relationships I've tolerated. Help me to seek You with my whole heart, with no reservations.

And Father, I pray for _____, that You might wake them up, spiritually speaking. Open their eyes to the reality that life is short and eternity is long. Impress on them the urgency of their own spiritual walk with You. And Father, I pray that the power of sin would be broken in their lives. May the value they place on their sins pale in comparison with the freedom and fulfillment that comes with submitting to Your sovereignty and direction.

Lord, if the first-century church in Rome needed to wake up to their reality, cause Christians today to realize all the more their need to wake up to the moral, spiritual, and religious deceptions happening around us. May we be faithful to serve You in acceptable ways.

In Jesus' name, Amen.

A Prayer That Our Enemies Be Brought to Justice

"My heart exults in the LORD; my horn is exalted in the LORD. My mouth derides my enemies, because I rejoice in your salvation... The adversaries of the LORD shall be broken to pieces; against them he will thunder in heaven."

—1 SAMUEL 2:1,10

Surprisingly, this prayer was offered to God in response to domestic rivalry. Hannah was bitterly treated by her husband's "other wife," who bore children, but Hannah herself was barren. Yes, in those days bigamy and even polygamy were tolerated by God. Of course this was never the ideal—God intended marriage to be between one man and one woman, as the creation account indicates. Indeed, the greatest argument in support of God's ideal arrangement is that in all the stories in the Old Testament where men had multiple wives, the arrangement ended with incredible domestic conflict!

Because being barren was considered a disgrace, Hannah felt the taunts of her rival very keenly. So when Hannah's prayer was answered and she gave birth to Samuel, she felt vindicated and asked God that her rival be judged for her disgraceful outbursts that had been aimed at her heart.

Today, think of someone who has purposefully wronged you or wronged someone you love. It is biblical to pray that God would reward them with just punishment. Often this means that their sin is exposed or that the evil they have done is returned on their own head. David prayed many such prayers against his enemies (see Psalms 35 and 109).

Of course, we do not seek vengeance, for that belongs to the Lord. We do not take matters into our own hands; we simply look to God to vindicate us in His own time and His own way. But praying this way affirms our confidence in God's ultimate justice. Whether now or later, the truth will win out and hidden evils will be exposed.

A Prayer to Begin Your Time of Intercession

Father, I pray for _____, that You might expose the evil done against _____ and that the perpetrator might be brought to repentance or else experience the pain he inflicted on others. Let him be unable to sleep; awaken him with the painful reality of what he has done and judge him accordingly. If granting him blessings will lead him to repentance, then I pray for his blessing. If it must be tragedy that awakens him to the trail of evil he has left behind, then do whatever is necessary to bring him to his senses.

Meanwhile give me the sure confidence that You will do what is right and good; let me entrust the evil done against me into Your sovereign hand, and with that, let me be content.

In Jesus' name, Amen.

A Plea for Faithfulness in Prayer

"Far be it from me that I should sin against the LORD
by ceasing to pray for you, and I will instruct you in the good
and the right way."

—1 SAMUEL 12:23

Do you have to confess the sin of prayerlessness? Samuel spoke the above words to the people of Israel, assuring them of his continual prayers on their behalf. He himself was born in answer to his mother's prayers, and as he grew up, he saw the value of prayer as he assumed his leadership position.

In contrast, Eli the priest, who had responsibility for the spiritual leadership of the nation, appears to have long since given up on prayer. In fact, when Samuel's mother came into the temple to pray that God would give her a son, Eli thought she was drunk! In Eli and Samuel we see a contrast between a cynical older man who had given up on prayer and a zealous younger man who knew both the privilege and responsibility of prayer.

Let us consider Samuel's words:

First, prayerlessness is not merely a weakness or an oversight—it is sin. We must realize that intercession—fervent praying—lies at the heart of God's pattern for getting His work done in the world. If prayerlessness is sin, we should not only begin a life of serious prayer; we should confess our neglect and treat our prayerlessness as we would any other sin.

Second, Samuel's prayers were selfless. He interceded not just for himself and his family, but for the nation of Israel. In context, the nation, which had insisted on having a human king rule over them, had run afoul of God's perfect will. Yet even though the people had crossed the line of disobedience, Samuel gave them hope on account of God's mercy and the faithfulness of those who still were praying on their behalf.

Finally, notice that Samuel's greatest fear was not that he might fail in public, but that he might fail in private—that is, he feared that he might stop praying. And he knew that if he failed in this private discipline, he would most assuredly fail in his public life as well. He connected prayer with his ability to instruct others "in the good and the right way."

We must pray for ourselves and for others, that a "culture of prayer" might be developed in our own lives that will give us both the desire and the discipline to pray and put our lives on the line for others. Let us believe that things will be different because we have prayed.

A Prayer to Begin Your Time of Intercession

Father, we confess our sin of prayerlessness. We admit that we have become cynical and indifferent, thinking that prayer will not change our circumstances or our nation. Help us to come to grips with the depth of our sin and the wonder of Your grace. Today we resolve to put our sin of prayerlessness behind us.

So we pray first for _____, who is in great need. We pray for their deliverance from the distress in which they find themselves. We pray that You will give them hope and peace.

Lord, like Samuel, who prayed for his nation, so we pray for ours. We confess we have separated You from law, from education, from science, and from the courts. We blush in shame for our many sins and rampant rebellion. Turn the hearts of people to You through our witness so that we, as a nation, might turn back to You.

In Jesus' name, Amen.

A Prayer for Purity of Motive

"Do not look on his appearance or on the height of his stature, because I have rejected him. For the LORD sees not as man sees: man looks on the outward appearance, but the LORD looks on the heart."

—1 SAMUEL 16:7

The context of this statement gives us insight into what God considers of utmost value. Samuel is asked by God to find another king for Israel, and is given specific instructions to go to the house of Jesse near Bethlehem because God was preparing one of Jesse's sons to be the next king. From the oldest to the youngest, the sons of Jesse strut past Samuel in hopes that they will be chosen for the position of fame and power. After the entire lineup passes by, Samuel is confused because none of the sons receives the nod of approval from God.

Samuel then asked Jesse if there are any other sons. It turns out there is one more. Jesse's youngest son, David, is brought to the prophet, and Samuel instantly recognizes him to be the the Lord's anointed. God made it clear that a man can be towering in stature and yet have a shriveled soul. A man can appear to have all the outward qualifications of leadership but have an unqualified heart. *When God measures a man, He puts the tape around the heart, not the head.*

What was it about David's heart that attracted God's attention?

David had a shepherd's heart—he was willing to take on bears and lions for the sake of the sheep. Now he would be the lead shepherd of the nation. He also gave evidence of humility, and despite the fame he gained for killing Goliath, he willingly became a servant to King Saul, the reigning king.

Best of all, David had a worshipping heart. He wrote many of the psalms, in which he cried out to God, longing for the divine presence and blessing, "As the deer pants for flowing streams, so pants my soul for you, O God. My soul thirsts for God, for the living God. When shall I come and appear before God?" (Psalm 42:1-2).

In his later years, David is primarily known for his forgiven heart. He had sinned deeply, grieving the God he loved. And in response, he poured out his heart to God, seeking His forgiveness and future blessing.

So when God measures a person, He doesn't look for outer beauty, He looks for inner integrity. He puts His stethoscope to the heart. We have to pray for hearts that are undivided in their focus and worship; we have to pray we will have hearts that long deeply for intimacy with God. It's not what others see, but the hidden parts of the heart that God sees that really matters.

A Prayer to Begin Your Time of Intercession

Father, I pray that You would give me a heart that is filled with love for You and others. Give me a heart that desires purity and spiritual wholeness; I pray that whatever You saw in David's heart, may it be found in mine.

Forgive me for having a divided heart. Forgive me for reserving a part of my heart for myself. Forgive my hypocrisy of living in a private world that contradicts my public world. May my heart properly fear Your name that I might live in a way that glorifies You.

Lord, I pray for _____, that they might repent of all that contaminates their heart. Let them give themselves to You for Your blessing without reservation or hesitation. Let Your grace work in them so that as You look upon them, You might be abundantly satisfied.

In Jesus' name, Amen.

Week 30

A Prayer That We Might Praise God Continually

"The LORD is my rock and my fortress and my deliverer, my God, my rock, in whom I take refuge, my shield, and the horn of my salvation, my stronghold and my refuge, my savior; you save me from violence. I call upon the LORD, who is worthy to be praised, and I am saved from my enemies."

—2 SAMUEL 22:2-4

This week let's concentrate on worshipping God with our praise.

There are times for us to intercede on behalf of others; there are times to pray for the sick, for finances, and for God's leading. And then there are times to simply cease asking and start praising. For the next seven days, let us devote ourselves to giving God the gratitude and the praise that He so richly deserves.

You have had the experience of fearing the worst, only to receive the good news that your fears were unfounded. You feared an exam and were so relieved when you discovered you'd made the grade. Or you've just been pronounced free of the cancer that was discovered a few months ago. Then again, you may have received some unexpected but much needed funds in the mail. Your heart is gladdened with joy and freedom.

David feared that Saul might kill him. For ten long years he ran from cave to cave and from village to village, staying ahead of the spies Saul had recruited to find him. Years of hiding, scrounging for food, and staying ahead of his murderers drained faith from his soul. So you can imagine David's relief when he was spared from the trap that Saul had laid for him.

Here is my proposal: Just as we give praise to God in moments of victory and deliverance, let us choose to praise Him similarly even when our future is uncertain. The reason we can do that is because we know that eventual relief from all of our cares is both certain and inevitable. We should say with David, "I will bless the LORD at all times; his praise shall continually be in my mouth" (Psalm 34:1).

Let this week be one of giving constant praise to God and limiting our requests to few in number. Pray through psalms of praise, such as Psalm 103 and Psalm 145. Let the Lord transform you through the power of praise!

A Prayer to Begin Your Time of Intercession

Father, let me continually give You unrestrained praise. I thank You that I am alive to serve You today; I praise Your name because You have counted me as Your own. Though Satan has attempted to destroy me, You have protected me and delivered me from his grasp. I bless You because Your promises are ever with me. And Your presence is above me, beneath me, and on all sides. I affirm that there is no circumstance that I must endure alone; by Your grace I want to give thanks in all things.

I pray for _____ and ask that You will help me to know how to motivate them to join me in giving You praise. Let us together believe that praise not only glorifies You; it also strengthens our faith and affirms that You are in charge of the whole universe and not just our small part of the world.

Help me to remember to give thanks in all things and offer prayers of adoration throughout this day.

In Jesus' name, Amen.

A Prayer That We Might Let God be God

"If I find favor in the eyes of the LORD, he will bring me back and let me see both it and his dwelling place. But if he says 'I have no pleasure in you,' behold, here I am, let him do to me what seems good to him."

—2 SAMUEL 15:25-26

Last week we joined David in giving praise to God for delivering him from Saul. Today I want to introduce you to a prayer that David uttered while in great despair. Yes, God delivered David from Saul, but now more ominously, the question was whether God would deliver him from the murderous intentions of his own son.

David's son, Absalom, rebelled against him, scheming to take the kingdom for himself. David's world was disintegrating by the hour. One hammer blow after another was smashing his life and kingdom to pieces. He had lost all moral authority to deal with his sons because of his own sin. He was forgiven by God, but he lost his leadership position within the family and never regained it. Even his friends were turning against him in public disrespect. His loyal advisor, Ahithophel, defected and joined Absalom, whose coup d'état was gaining an ever-widening following.

As things went from bad to worse, David had to flee Jerusalem, leaving his scattered family and disintegrating kingdom behind. A man named Shimei even had the audacity to throw stones at the departing king and curse him as he was going up the Mount of Olives. One of David's soldiers volunteered to take off Shimei's head, but David would have none of it. "Leave him alone, and let him curse, for the LORD has told him to," David said (2 Samuel 16:11). David was keenly aware of his failure in all this, so he was willing to accept whatever happened. Even Shimei's curses against David were interpreted as coming from the hand of God.

There was no fight left in David. The prayer he prayed as he left the city was one of total brokenness and helplessness. Years earlier, he did not manipulate events to get the kingdom from Saul prematurely, and now, he would not scheme to keep it in his hands. If his own life could be spared, fine; indeed, he was willing to lead his troops to battle against his own son. But David was a broken man. The kingdom meant nothing to him now. His many wives were whispering behind his back, and one of his sons was out to kill him. He was being crushed by God, and he accepted it.

Contrary to David's wishes, Absalom was killed, and yes, David did return to Jerusalem to rule. But nothing would ever be the same again. David would live long enough to see outsiders plot to steal the kingdom and then witness the tragic deaths of two more of his sons.

When it came time for David to die, he had nothing left but God.

Let us pray with the same resignation, believing that all things are best left in God's hands.

A Prayer to Begin Your Time of Intercession

Father, when we find ourselves at the end of our rope only to discover that there is no knot on the end, help us to cling to Your promises. When we discover that all hope is gone, help us to take one last look at You, committing ourselves entirely into Your hands. Lord, may the struggle within our souls cease; may we no longer try to manipulate events that are out of our control. If You do not help us, we will not be helped; if You do not deliver us, we will not be delivered.

I pray this not only for myself but also for _____. May they be wholly yielded to Your will and purpose. We are like a piece of driftwood on a river whose speed and direction we cannot control. Yet we know that You have this river in Your hands. Help us to trust that You will do right by us; give us the assurance that when You are our only hope, that is sufficient and we need nothing more. Only Your will and glory matters. To that end we dedicate ourselves.

In Jesus' name, Amen.

A Prayer About All We Possess in Christ

"Because of him [God] you are in Christ Jesus, who became
to us wisdom from God, righteousness and sanctification
and redemption, so that, as it is written, 'Let the one who
boasts, boast in the Lord.'"

—1 CORINTHIANS 1:30-31

When we think about Christ's relationship with us, we immediately think of what He did for us as our substitute, bearing our sin on the cross. But He is not only our sin-bearer, He also embodies all that we need for our continuing spiritual growth and strength to face all of life. In other words, the better we see Jesus, the better we will strive to be all that we can be for His glory. Larry Crabb said it well: "Unbelievers do not see Christ as their greatest treasure. Neither do most believers…More is available to us in Christ than we dare imagine. We settle for so much less. We taste Him so little."[7]

Let's meditate on the four blessings Paul mentions here.

Do you need *wisdom* for discernment and knowing God's will? We can be sure that if we seek Christ in His fullness we will have that wisdom; we will especially have the wisdom to better understand the glory of the gospel and the riches we have stored up for us.

Have you sunk into discouragement because you have sinned—*again*? Remember that Jesus is still your *righteousness* before the Father, and He represents you in heaven.

Are you discouraged at the lack of personal victory in your walk with God? In Christ, we are set apart; we are made holy. He is our *sanctifier* who is constantly working out our salvation both through trials and through the application of His Word.

And finally, are you feeling as if you don't count, and that you're of no value to anyone? Christ is our *redemption*; He purchased us for the Father at great personal cost. Thanks to His undeserved mercy toward us, He redeemed us with His own blood and sees us as His inheritance (Ephesians 1:18). No matter how we devalue ourselves, in God's sight we are highly honored and accepted in Jesus, His Beloved One.

Let us ask God to quicken our minds so that we might catch a glimpse of the wonder of who Christ is and the blessings He brings to us!

A Prayer to Begin Your Time of Intercession

Father, I pray that You might help us to understand that we need Jesus more than we need food and drink and a place to sleep. We need Him more than life itself. Help us to see Him as our very life; we pray that giving Him honor might be our greatest desire. May the blessed Holy Spirit show us the practical application of the wonderful truths in 1 Corinthians 1:30-31.

I pray for _____, that they might see Jesus as more compelling than the allurement of sin. I pray that they'll see that Jesus gives us eternal realities, that He is to us what we need every moment. I pray that all of us might have a greater passion for Him than we have to sin. Wisdom, righteousness, sanctification, and redemption cause us to better understand what is entailed in these blessings and how they should impact us each day.

In Jesus' name, Amen.

Prayer puts God's work in His hands—and keeps it there.

E.M. Bounds

A Prayer About Appearing at the Judgment Seat of Christ

*"Now if anyone builds on the foundation with gold, silver,
precious stones, wood, hay, straw—each one's work will become
manifest, for the Day will disclose it, because it
will be revealed by fire, and the fire will test what sort of
work each one has done."*

—1 Corinthians 3:12-13

All believers will appear before the Judgment Seat of Christ to give account of themselves to God. Let us suppose that every deed we've done since our conversion is turned into either a piece of precious metal or a piece of straw depending on the quality of the work. Then let us imagine that our works are torched so that when we stand next to Jesus, we will see for ourselves how fruitful (or *un*fruitful) we were in this life.

In fact, I'm told that a man had just such a dream. In it, Jesus took the man's works and lit them. The fire burned brightly, and when it was over, he noticed that there were bits of metal that survived the flames. With a small brush he swept these tiny pieces of gold and silver into his hand.

What will Jesus be looking for on the day we stand before Him?

Evidently the precious metals represent desirable qualities, such as the joyful acceptance of injustice (Matthew 5:11-12), financial generosity toward the things of God (Matthew 6:19-21), hospitality (Luke 14:12-14), loving the unlovable (Luke 6:32-36), etc.

Let us pray that we all will have precious metals that will survive the fire.

A Prayer to Begin Your Time of Intercession

Father, we pray that You will so purify our motives that we might bring You honor in the day that we're judged by Your blessed Son. Forgive us for piling up massive amounts of wood, hay, and straw that won't survive the flames. Make us dissatisfied with the temporal; give us an irrepressible desire to see You glorified in our thought life so that everything we do is a credit to Your redemption and love for us.

I pray for _____, that they might not live for themselves but for Jesus, who redeemed them. I pray that they might desire to do well at the Judgment Seat of Christ for Your honor and glory. I pray that pleasing You might be more important to them than pleasing themselves. Let them grasp the fact that how we do at the Judgment Seat determines how much responsibility we will be entrusted with in the coming kingdom. I pray for myself and all who are on my heart and mind…O God, give us hearts that desire only Your praise!

In Jesus' name, Amen.

A Prayer for Purity

"Your boasting is not good. Do you not know that a little leaven leavens the whole lump? Cleanse out the old leaven that you may be a new lump, as you really are unleavened. For Christ, our Passover lamb, has been sacrificed."

—1 Corinthians 5:6-7

"Or do you not know that your body is a temple of the Holy Spirit within you, whom you have from God? You are not your own, for you were bought with a price. So glorify God in your body."

—1 Corinthians 6:19-20

Sin—particularly known sin—weakens the church.

In context, Paul is chastising the church at Corinth because the people there had allowed at least one immoral relationship to continue without disciplining the offenders. Paul chides the church for not mourning over this moral failure, but rather continuing with business as usual and even bragging about how great their church was. But God will not stand by without some form of discipline and judgment of His own. And in such a case, the whole church suffers. Public sin must have some kind of public discipline.

Someone once said that the most quoted verse in the Bible is not John 3:16, but Matthew 7:1: "Judge not, that you be not judged." This verse is interpreted to mean that church leaders should never judge anyone who continues in sin. After all, we're all sinners, so who are we to judge? But Jesus' words in Matthew 7:1 certainly do *not* mean that we should tolerate sins such as deceit and immorality among believers. In that passage, Jesus was talking to the Pharisees, or religious leaders who judged others but refused to judge themselves. He wanted them to judge themselves first and deal with the sin in their lives before they put themselves in a position to judge others.

When Paul urged the church in Corinth to "cleanse out the old leaven," he was referring to the Old Testament instruction that the Passover meal should not be eaten as long as there was leaven in the house—for the bread at the feast was to be unleavened. Indeed, before the Passover meal, the Jews went through an elaborate ritual of searching their houses for the slightest hint of leaven so they could remove it. Leaven is a picture of sin; a small lump of leaven can work secretly and puff up the dough so that it spreads and affects the entire loaf of bread. Just so, when we tolerate sin in a church, like yeast, it works secretly to affect the whole congregation.

Let us pray that sin will be revealed and dealt with biblically so that our churches will be free to grow and be an effective witness for Jesus Christ.

A Prayer to Begin Your Time of Intercession

Father, we admit that we are a sinful people; we admit that we often sin in thought, word, and deed. We pray that You might cleanse us first, no matter how painful it may be. We pray for the leadership of our churches; help them to live holy lives so that they might have the courage to deal with sin among the members of their congregations. We pray that You might reveal immoral relationships, deceitful practices, and sinful attitudes that exist among our leadership.

I pray for _____, that they might live in submission to those who have authority over them, whether it's their parents or the leaders of the church. Help us all to be accountable to someone and be willing to accept rebuke when it's offered in love for our own good. We pray that overt sin will be exposed; we ask, Lord, that our churches might be filled with those whose private lives match their public persona.

Rid all of us of the hypocrisy of living in two worlds. Make us a genuine people who are submissive to those who look out for our good. Yes, Lord, come to cleanse Your church.

In Jesus' name, Amen.

A Prayer to Resist Temptation

"No temptation has overtaken you that is not common to man. God is faithful, and he will not let you be tempted beyond your ability, but with the temptation he will also provide the way of escape, that you may be able to endure it."

—1 CORINTHIANS 10:13

On one occasion, a Christian woman came to the elders of our church and asked for special prayer because she was so terribly tempted to accept the pressure from her male friend that they become sexually intimate. Because immorality had been in her background, she found herself weary of resisting his overtures and was about to give in to the temptation. We admired the fact that she was willing to seek out special prayer when she felt she was being tested above what she could bear.

In the verses leading up to 1 Corinthians 10:13, the apostle Paul wrote about the sins of the Israelites, who, though greatly blessed by God, nonetheless succumbed to sins of various kinds: idolatry, sexual immorality, grumbling, anger, and the like. They were released from slavery in Egypt, they were led by God in the desert, and their needs were cared for. Yet in the face of all these undeserved privileges and provisions, they turned their back on the God who loved them. Their sin was greater because their opportunities were greater.

The verse we are using this week for our prayer time is a promise with this assurance: God gives us shoulders that are strong enough to bear whatever He places on them. We cannot use our backgrounds, those who have wronged us, or our circumstances as excuses for sinning. With the test comes a way of escape so that we can bear it. As someone once said, "God doesn't give us what we can handle; God helps us handle what we are given."

The people in the church at Corinth could not excuse sin in their midst because of their cultural situation (Corinth was renowned for its many prostitutes and rampant sexual immorality). God requires holiness no matter what temptations a church is surrounded with; an evil world never justifies an evil church. Unfortunately, some of the church's members were looking for relief from their temptations through indulgence, not endurance.

We can have confidence that God will give us, and those we love, the grace and strength to find a way of escape in the midst of our temptations. Often that way of escape is to flee from the very presence of the temptation. We must be willing to break away from our television, leave a sinful relationship, or move to another part of town. In other words, we should do whatever is necessary for us to avoid the temptations that erode our ability to resist sin's enticements.

A Prayer to Begin Your Time of Intercession

Father, I pray that You might deliver me from the excuses I use to justify my sin. Help me to realize that no matter how severe the test, You offer me the grace I need to endure it. Help me to find the way of escape and teach others so that they also can find the route to victory and blessing.

I pray for _____, that they might be willing to pay any price to keep from stumbling into sin. I pray that they might realize that regardless of the test they are experiencing, someone else in the same circumstances, and with the same desires, met that same test successfully. I pray that they might find a way of escape, that they might find the door that will lead them away from the temptation rather than toward it. Deliver them from those clever rationalizations that we so often use in order to justify our sin.

Thank You that Jesus endured this trial successfully, and that because He stands in our place, He can help us do the same.

In Jesus' name, Amen.

A Prayer for the Discernment to Make Wise Choices

"Give your servant therefore an understanding mind to govern your people, that I may discern between good and evil, for who is able to govern this your great people?"

—1 KINGS 3:9

At the beginning of his long reign, God gave Solomon an invitation to ask for whatever he wanted. "Ask what I shall give you," the Lord told him (1 Kings 3:5). Solomon prayed for the gift of wisdom—the gift of discernment or the ability to make the best choice when confronted with a number of options. God then commended Solomon for not asking for a long life, nor riches, nor for the life of his enemies, but rather for requesting an understanding heart. God was very pleased and promised that Solomon would get what he asked for.

Today, we still benefit from Solomon's wisdom when we read the book of Proverbs, most of which was written by him.

Cleary, God takes delight in giving us wisdom when we are confronted with difficult choices. I've discovered that He gladly grants wisdom even in impromptu situations, such as when I'm talking on the phone and I silently claim the promise, "If any of you lacks wisdom, let him ask God, who gives generously to all without reproach, and it will be given him" (James 1:5). No matter what our situation, God is pleased to give us the wisdom we need at a given particular moment.

There are, however, some basic requirements for having our prayer answered. First, James says we have to ask in faith—we have to believe that God will actually give wisdom as generously as He has promised. Wavering unbelief only perpetuates repetitive uncertainty.

Second, it's clear that we have to be willing to obey the wisdom God gives us. I've frequently asked seemingly mismatched couples if they had sought God's wisdom before they got married. Often they respond, "No, we just assumed it was God's will." Or, they acknowledge that they didn't ask for wisdom because they feared that God would say no to what they wanted to do.

When we fail to ask for wisdom, we leave ourselves vulnerable to making poor decisions. Tragically, that must have been the case with Solomon, for later in life he himself turned away from the Lord and chose the path of sensual desire rather than the more difficult and honorable path of wisdom.

Now comes a key question: How does God's wisdom come to us? The wise path is, first and foremost, made known to us through the Scriptures. Beyond that, wisdom comes through peace in our minds and hearts that we're doing the right thing. Another way that wisdom comes to us is through the counsel of another person whom God puts in our path. Often wisdom is simply a matter of making a decision in faith and giving God an opportunity to stop us if we are wrong. He can close or open doors as He leads those who are willing to be led.

Let us pray for wisdom whenever we or others are faced with difficult decisions.

A Prayer to Begin Your Time of Intercession

Father, I pray that You would give me a heart of wisdom. I pray that I will seek to always make wise choices. And when two paths seem to be equal, I pray You will help me to trust You even as I make my decision. Give me a heart that is willing to obey You, to respond in faith to the wisdom You give me.

I pray for _____, that they might have a heart of wisdom. Keep them from ungodly counsel that seems good but, in the end, will be destructive. Keep them from following the path of least resistance and from friends who would lead them astray. Teach them, even as You teach me, that the wise path is often the most difficult one, but that in the end, it's the most rewarding.

Direct our paths, O Lord, for we are like sheep who are prone to stray. Make us lovers of wisdom.

In Jesus' name, Amen.

A Prayer for Faith in Desperate Circumstances

"O our God, will you not execute judgment on them? For we are powerless against this great horde that is coming against us. We do not know what to do, but our eyes are on you."

—2 Chronicles 20:12

Imagine being responsible not only for your own fate, but also the fate of a nation. That's the predicament Jehoshaphat found himself in when a great army was moving against the land of Judah. Filled with fear, he "set his face to seek the Lord" (2 Chronicles 20:3) and called the people together to fast and pray for God's mercy and protection. He prayed earnestly, confessing his sin and the sin of his people, reminding himself of God's greatness and His covenant with His chosen people. Jehoshaphat understood that he was no match for the overwhelming superiority of the armies headed his way. If there was to be deliverance, God would have to directly intervene.

This prayer of desperation was also accompanied by worship. "Then Jehoshaphat bowed his head with his face to the ground, and all Judah and the inhabitants of Jerusalem fell down before the Lord, worshiping the Lord" (verse 18). Next, Jehoshaphat turned military strategy on its head by sending a choir ahead of his own army! Should we be surprised when we read, "When they began to sing and praise, the Lord set an ambush against the men of Ammon, Moab, and Mount Seir, who had come against Judah, so that they were routed" (verse 22)?

There are lessons here for us when we are in a desperate place. First, God can use whatever means He wishes to deliver us. He can thwart armies and reverse whatever seems to be coming at us. He is never in need of ideas to help us.

Second—and perhaps this is most important—God answers when we ask in faith, a faith fueled by worship. One of the best things we can do when we're in a frightful place is to pause and give praise to God with singing and the affirmation of His promises. Desperate prayer that is unaccompanied by praise is almost always a prayer of unbelief. Praise always captures God's ear—and prompts His response.

A Prayer to Begin Your Time of Intercession

Father, teach me to praise You at all times, particularly when I am confronted by my enemies. I have deep-seated fears within my soul about my future, my health, and especially about those whose greatest delight would be to witness my destruction. Lord, today I turn away from those fears to give You praise. Like the choir that led the armies of Judah into battle, I move forward with praise and gratitude for Your great name and the power of Your love.

I pray for _____, that they might develop the habit of giving You praise each morning; I pray that they might read the psalms of praise, giving You their thanks and worship. Teach them, even as You teach me, that when we don't know what to do, praise is always the right response. Together let us quote the words of Jehoshaphat's choir: "Give thanks to the LORD, for his steadfast love endures forever" (verse 21). May Your praise be continually on our lips.

In Jesus' name, Amen.

A Prayer That Our Hearts Be Open to God's Word

"Ezra had set his heart to study the Law of the LORD, and to do it and to teach his statutes and rules in Israel."
—EZRA 7:10

"All the people wept as they heard the words of the Law."
—NEHEMIAH 8:9

Ezra was a scribe who set himself to "study the Law of the LORD and to do it." Later, we read that he instructed Israel, and thankfully, the people had ears to listen to what God was saying. This stands in contrast to a past generation of Israelites who had refused to listen to the words of the Lord as proclaimed through the prophets. They might have heard the words, but they dismissed them out of hand. As the old saying goes, no one is as deaf as the person who does not want to hear.

What are the characteristics of those who are ready to hear God's Word? First, they listen to His Word with anticipation, wanting to be instructed. In fact, they love hearing the Word of God even when it rebukes them. They have an appetite for spiritual things and, "like newborn infants, long for the pure spiritual milk" (1 Peter 2:2) so that they might grow in their walk with God. In other words, they're eager to be both comforted and confronted by the Word.

Second, they are willing to hear the Word despite the competition from other voices. Above the noise of this world, they pick out the voice of the True Shepherd and follow wherever He leads.

When the Pentagon was hit and severely damaged during the 9/11 terrorist attacks, the building was filled with dense smoke. A man near an exit door called out to his fellow employees who couldn't see through the smoke, directing them to safety. Though they could see nothing, they groped their way toward the direction of his voice and were able to reach safety. Just so, we are in a world that is very lost, confused, and without direction. The Word of God calls out to us, giving us hope and direction amid the chaos. But if we insist on listening to another voice, we will do so to our peril.

A Prayer to Begin Your Time of Intercession

Father, I pray that I would always be ready to hear Your voice. May I be eager to hear what You have to say to me through Your written Word, and by the Word as it is preached and sung at church. Lord, there are some things in Your Word that are difficult to hear—warnings about the need for purity and the need for genuine repentance from sin. Let me be willing to hear those words and obey them.

I pray for _____, that they might not turn away from the truth, but instead would listen intently to what You are saying to them. Lord, it appears that at times the voices of this world are louder than Your still small voice; help them to discern that the loudest voice is not always the wisest voice. Open their spiritual ears, I pray; help them to hear You calling them by name to be Yours both now and forever.

In Jesus' name, Amen.

A Prayer for Our Nation

*"As soon as I heard these words I sat down and wept and
mourned for days, and I continued fasting and praying before
the God of heaven. And I said, 'O LORD God of heaven, the
great and awesome God who keeps covenant and steadfast love
with those who love him and keep his commandments, let your
ear be attentive and your eyes open, to hear the prayer of your
servant that I now pray before you day and night for the people
of Israel your servants, confessing the sins of the people of Israel,
which we have sinned against you. Even I and my father's house
have sinned. We have acted very corruptly against you and have
not kept the commandments, the statutes, and the rules that
you commanded your servant Moses.'...O LORD, let your ear be
attentive to the prayer of your servant, and to the prayer of your
servants who delight to fear your name, and give success to your
servant today, and grant him mercy in the sight of this man."*

—NEHEMIAH 1:4-7,11

This is the prayer of Nehemiah before he left Babylon to return to
Jerusalem to help rebuild the walls that had been destroyed by
conquering armies. The remnant of Jews who had survived the siege
of the city were dispirited and living in great trouble and shame. They
were constantly subject to attack from invaders who looted the city and
kept the Jews in humiliation. As far as this remnant was concerned,
no one cared about them, and they lost their testimony and impact.

All of this weighed heavily on Nehemiah's heart. He could have
dismissed the plight of these Jews as their problem, not his. But he
cared about his fellow Jews and the witness of God that had been lost
in the city. So he prayed for Jerusalem, knowing that until the people
had confessed their sins, they could not come to God for help. His
prayer acknowledged not just the sins of the present populace, but also

the sins of their forefathers, whose judgment had led to the destruction of the city.

This week, let us adapt Nehemiah's prayer to our own country, regardless of where we live. Let us repeatedly read this prayer before God as an indication of our own personal repentance and the need for our repentance as a nation. Yes, we should confess personal sin, but Nehemiah's prayer serves as an example of how we can also pray for the sins of our country.

A Prayer to Begin Your Time of Intercession

Father, today I pray for our nation. O God, we have sinned greatly. And not just we, but also the generations preceding us. (At this point, pray Nehemiah's prayer, adapting it to our country.)

In Jesus' name, Amen.

A Prayer That We Recognize Our Place in God's Plans

"Do not think to yourself that in the king's palace you will escape any more than all the other Jews. For if you keep silent at this time, relief and deliverance will rise for the Jews from another place, but you and your father's house will perish. And who knows whether you have not come to the kingdom for such a time as this?"

—ESTHER 4:13-14

These are the words of Mordecai to Esther, the young woman whom Mordecai had adopted after her parents died. Through divine providence, she was selected by King Ahasuerus to replace his rebellious wife Vashti, and so Esther had access to the king. And when the king unwittingly agreed to a plot to kill all the Jews in his kingdom, it was Esther who intervened, and the plot was averted. Indeed, she had "come to the kingdom for such a time as this."

Our role in life is probably not as dramatic as the role Esther played. But make no mistake—we also are where we are at this time in history to play an important role in God's eternal plan. You and I could have been born in a different era, or we could have been born in a different country, with different parents and a radically different environment. But we are who we are at this place and time in history "for such a time as this."

We all know that, according to Ephesians 2:8-9, we are saved by grace through faith, and that this is not of our own doing, but rather, it is the gift of God. But the next verse reads, "For we are his workmanship, created in Christ Jesus for good works, which God prepared beforehand that we would walk in them" (verse 10).

You and I are God's workmanship created for this hour in history. Our parents, our upbringing—whether positive or negative—can be redeemed by God's gracious power so that we can serve Him effectively *today*. Our gifts, talents, and even our appearance are freely given to us by God, and they are to be used for God's glory. Envy is a sin because it charges God with unfairness and reveals our unwillingness to accept who and where we are by divine providence.

Are you content with who you are? Do you believe that God can redeem your past so that you can serve Him right now, wherever you might be? Are you angry at "the card you have been dealt," as one person put it?

Let us confess the sin of discontentment and pray that God will help us see that we have a role to play in His kingdom, and that we were born "for such a time as this."

A Prayer to Begin Your Time of Intercession

Father, I pray that I might truly believe that I have been saved with the distinct purpose of serving You with works You have marked out for me. I am Your creation, intended by You to carry out Your plan within my family, my neighborhood, and my country. I am Yours to be used as You will.

I pray for _____, that they might accept their lot in life; I pray that they might not envy those who have a more prominent position nor despise those who appear to have a lesser role in life. I pray that no task would be too lowly nor too obscure, but that they might see it as an opportunity to serve You.

Let us be content with where You have planted us, believing that we are created for today and that we are being led by Your hand. We are here "for such a time as this."

In Jesus' name, Amen.

Turn the Bible into prayer.

Robert Murray M'Cheyne

A Prayer to Understand Our Identity in Christ

*"I have been crucified with Christ. It is no longer I who live,
but Christ who lives in me. And the life I now live in the
flesh I live by faith in the Son of God, who loved me
and gave himself for me."*

—GALATIANS 2:20

The changes God makes in our lives after our conversion are profound and lasting; He does a deep work that rituals cannot perform. Consider this: God so profoundly put us into Jesus—in a legal way—that His history becomes our history. We were crucified with Him, and will be raised as He was (see Romans 6:5). This identification with Christ is the basis for our intimate relationship with Him; it is also the basis of our walk of victory.

If you were convicted of a capital crime and then put to death for it, the law would have no more claim on you. Just so, as believers, we've died with Christ, and as a result, we are dead to our obligations to meet the demands of the law. In short, Jesus fulfilled the demands of the law for us. So our "death" with Jesus frees us from a standard we could never keep and the punishments that accompany it. Yet—thanks be to God—we still do live, but we do so by faith in Jesus.

"The true Christian life," writes John MacArthur, "is not so much a believer's living for Christ as Christ's living through the believer."[8] Before our conversion, we did the best we could at managing our guilt and hoping that we could rectify our relationship with God. After our conversion, we continue to strive, but with an entirely different motivation: Now we're empowered by letting Christ live in and through us. Our responsibility is to surrender with confidence so that the life we now live we live by faith in the Son of God, who loved us and gave Himself for us.

This "crucified life," as it is sometimes called, means that we not only died to the law in Christ, but we must, by faith, die to our own plans and ambitions. Our lives are now entirely in His capable hands. Letting Christ live in us opens up a whole spectrum of hope and victory.

We are saved by faith in Christ who died for us; now we continue to have faith in the Christ who lives for us and in us. Today, let us not concentrate as much on living for Christ as trusting Christ to live in us! And let us pray we will understand and obey.

A Prayer to Begin Your Time of Intercession

Father, I begin by asking that I will grasp the meaning of Galatians 2:20, which says the demands of the law have been met on my behalf by Jesus Christ. And equally wonderful is the truth that Jesus now lives in me. Let me exercise the same faith in the living Christ within me as I have for the dying Christ who died for me. Let the thought that Christ lives within me captivate my mind and heart such that I live every moment in the light of this truth.

Then, Father, I also pray for _____, that rather than live for self, they might submit to Jesus. And if they do not know Him as Savior, I pray that they will receive His gift of grace and accept Him as their Savior and Lord. Father, do a work in their heart that is miraculous and lasting.

Father, help me to believe that Christ living within me frees me from stress and the senseless pressures of life. Take charge in me, and work through me for Your glory.

In Jesus' name, Amen.

A Prayer About Our Riches in Christ

*"I do not cease to give thanks for you, remembering you in
my prayers, that the God of our Lord Jesus Christ, the Father of
glory, may give you the Spirit of wisdom and of revelation in the
knowledge of him, having the eyes of your hearts enlightened,
that you may know what is the hope to which he has
called you, what are the riches of his glorious inheritance in
the saints, and what is the immeasurable greatness of his power
toward us who believe."*

—Ephesians 1:16-19

Have you ever prayed for something—perhaps for someone to
be healed—and then ended your prayer by saying, "If it is Your
will"? I believe that's the proper way to pray, especially when we're not
sure whether or not our request is in line with what God wants to do.
When Jesus was in Gethsemane, He prayed to the Father, "Not my
will, but yours, be done" (Luke 22:42). However, there are times when
we can pray without specifying "If it is Your will" because we already
know that we are praying in line with God's will—in other words, we
are praying God's will *exactly*.

That's what happens, for example, when we pray the prayers of
the apostle Paul, who spent a great deal of time praying for others. His
prayers, which appear in Scripture, always expressed God's desire for
His people.

Please reread Paul's prayer in Ephesians 1:16-19 and notice what he
did *not* pray for. He did not ask that the believers in Ephesus be made
rich, or that they be healed physically, or even that they might be kept

from suffering and persecution. When we pray such prayers—and those requests might be appropriate at times—we should add "If it is Your will" for the simple reason that we do not know whether these matters are God's desire or not. But when we pray for the spiritual realities for which Paul prayed, then we know that we are praying God's will back to Him. What Paul requested in Ephesians 6:16-19 is God's will for all of His people in all ages.

This prayer we are considering is among the grandest that we could ever pray for ourselves and others. Even if we prayed this prayer each day, we could never exhaust its depths, and we would immediately see that we are always in need of these realities 24/7.

There's a story about how the wealthy newspaper publisher William Randolph Hearst once read about an extremely valuable piece of art that he thought should be added to his extensive collection. He instructed his agent to find it and pay for it at any price. After a painstaking search, the agent reported that it was found in Hearst's own warehouse and it had already been his for many years!

Just so, most of the blessings we pray for are already part of our inheritance as God's children. And along with Paul, we should pray that all believers might understand what they already have been given in Christ—the power and the experiences they have been longing for already belong to them.

This week, take your Bible and read the entire prayer (Ephesians 1:15-23) every single day; read it for different people, first for yourself, then for your family, and then for your church. You will discover unexpected strength and blessing from reading this prayer back to God. And in the end, you do not have to say, "If it be Your will"!

A Prayer to Begin Your Time of Intercession

Father, I thank You for the apostle Paul, who not only had a burden to pray for Your people, but also, by divine relation, understood what Your will is for each of us. So I pray that You might now give me freedom in praying this prayer for _____, that they might come to experience all the blessings that belong to us by faith in Christ.

Lord, expand the vision and understanding of _____ as I pray for them from this rich treasure of Your Word—I do not cease to give thanks for you, remembering you in my prayers...(read Ephesians 1:15-23).

In Jesus' name, Amen.

A Prayer That We Fully Understand God's Power and Love

*"For this reason I bow my knees before the Father, from whom
every family in heaven and on earth is named, that according to the riches of his glory he may grant you to be strengthened
with power through his Spirit in your inner being, so that Christ
may dwell in your hearts through faith—that you, being rooted
and grounded in love, may have strength to comprehend with
all the saints what is the breadth and length and height and
depth, and to know the love of Christ that surpasses knowledge,
that you may be filled with all the fullness of God. Now to him
who is able to do far more abundantly than all that we ask or
think, according to the power at work within us, to him be glory
in the church and in Christ Jesus throughout all generations,
forever and ever. Amen."*

—EPHESIANS 3:14-21

Here is another prayer we should pray often for ourselves and others. As we learned in the previous prayer, Paul did not pray for the physical well-being of the believers at Ephesus, however impor-tant that was. Rather, he gave his attention to praying that they might experience both the power and love of God.

Notice the following features of this prayer. First, he prayed that all the believers would be strengthened in the "inner man"—that place within each of us that can only be changed by the power of God. Although the outer man grows weaker over time, the inner man can be renewed day by day. This is a reference to the innermost depths of our being, where the Spirit resides and does His work.

Second, Paul prayed that that "Christ may dwell in your hearts through faith." At first blush we might think this is a strange prayer for Christians to pray because Christ already dwells in our hearts. Indeed, Paul repeatedly made it clear in his epistles that all believers are in Christ. But the Greek term translated "dwell" does not just mean that Christ is present, but rather, that He is at home in our hearts. The question for every believer is this: Does Jesus reside in your heart as a tolerated visitor or as an honored and most welcome guest?

D.A. Carson writes, "Make no mistake: when Christ first moves into our lives, He finds it in very bad repair."[9] As soon as He takes up residence in us, the Lord begins His work.

In his booklet *My Heart—Christ's Home*, Robert Munger pictures our heart as Jesus' home.[10] When He comes to dwell in us, our Lord goes from room to room, visiting the library (our minds), the dining room (where our desires reside), the living room (where we invite our guests to stay), and even the closets, where we hide our sins from the prying eyes of others. Jesus, in making this tour, sadly finds that our "house" is inhabited with many selfish desires and sinful "guests." And He insists that we give Him the keys to the closets of our hearts so that He can help cleanse us, throw out the trash, and begin to feel at home in our hearts.

The more comfortable Christ is in our hearts, the better we will grasp the love of God in all of its breadth, length, height, and depth. When we honor Christ, all of this is fulfilled in our lives.

As you pray the following prayer, you may want to say it out loud for emphasis. Of course this is not for God's benefit; He can hear the faintest whisper. Rather it's for your benefit, as saying a prayer out loud can help you to concentrate and focus on it better.

A Prayer to Begin Your Time of Intercession

Father, I pray that I would willingly open every part of my heart and let Christ renovate it so that He might feel very much at home within me. I give Him the key to every room—I invite Him into my mind, my emotions, and even into the closets where I have hidden my secret sins. Father, for this I need Your divine power.

And I pray for _____, who also needs to let Christ be at home in their life. I ask that Jesus would not only be welcomed, but feel truly at home in their heart.

And now I pray with Paul…(read Ephesians 3:14-21).

In Jesus' name, Amen.

A Prayer That We Honor Christ

*"It is my prayer that your love may abound more and
more, with knowledge and all discernment, so that you may
approve what is excellent, and so be pure and blameless for
the day of Christ, filled with the fruit of righteousness that
comes through Jesus Christ, to the glory and praise of God."*
—PHILIPPIANS 1:9-11

Today we come to the prayer that I personally pray for each of my grandchildren individually each week. If this prayer were answered, it would encompass the hopes and dreams of any parent or grandparent. No prayer covers so much of what is essential for all of us in our walk with God. Obviously, because this prayer is present in Scripture, we can know that it is fully in line with God's perfect will.

Love is the supreme virtue in Christianity; love for God and others sums up the heart of the Law, and God's intention for us all. Love comes from God, for "God is love"—thus it is birthed by the blessed Holy Spirit of God within us. For our love to "abound more and more" is a prayer that we might be more like God.

Note also that this love abounds "with knowledge and all discernment." That is, we are to have a sure knowledge of the Scriptures and God's truth, and we are to have discernment, which includes the ability to apply God's revelation to the issues of life. Today, this is more important than ever. Clear insight into the reality of a situation is what Paul prays for.

Paul also prays that we might be "pure and blameless for the day of Christ"—that we live without moral failure and keep ourselves separated from the sins of the world which abound all around us. In an age of technology that makes moral breakdown easier than ever before, we need the spiritual and moral strength to live the pure and holy lives God calls us to.

To be "filled with the fruit of righteousness" is, of course, an extension of what it means to be pure and holy. We are to allow the Holy Spirit to have His way in our hearts so He can produce the fruit that is so special to God.

Finally, we're to do all these things "to the glory and praise of God." We're to do them with the single motive of giving God glory. Indeed, our only motive should be to give God the praise that He deserves.

Pray this inspired prayer every day this week. Memorize it and meditate on its profound beauty and godly aspirations. Pray it for yourself and for others. You will be blessed, and God will be honored.

A Prayer to Begin Your Time of Intercession

Father, thank You for giving us the resources to live extraordinary and supernatural lives that bring praise to Your name. And now, I pray Paul's prayer for myself…(pray the entire prayer in Philippians 1:9-11).

I pray as well for _____, that they might be kept by Your divine power and that their love may abound…(repeat the prayer in Philippians 1:9-11).

In Jesus' name, Amen.

A Prayer for Hope

*"Oh, that I knew where I might find him, that I might come
even to his seat! I would lay my case before him and fill my
mouth with arguments...Behold, I go forward, but he is not
there, and backward, but I do not perceive him; on the left hand
when he is working, I do not behold him; he turns to the right
hand, but I do not see him. But he knows the way that I take;
when he has tried me, I shall come out as gold."*

—JOB 23:3-4,8-10

Job felt abandoned by God, and his grief was increased as he listened to the rebuke coming from his three so-called friends. Their argument was simple: For Job to have lost his children and his health meant that he had sinned against God and deserved his fate. So they set out to help Job uncover his transgression and confess it. Only then, they reasoned, would he be blessed again by God. For his part, Job did not claim to be perfect, but he simply did not agree that he was the sinner that his friends had made him out to be.

Even after all the tragedy he faced and burying his ten children, Job remained faithful in his worship of God. His wife was of no help, however. She urged him to "curse God and die" (Job 2:9). But after sitting on an ash heap day after day with painful boils all over his body, Job's faith began to wane—especially in the face of the unrelenting criticism from his three friends, who kept probing his soul to find the source of his tragedy.

In despair Job cried, "God gives me up to the ungodly and casts me into the hands of the wicked. I was at ease, and he broke me apart; he seized me by the neck and dashed me to pieces; he set me up as his target; his archers surround me. He slashes open my kidneys and does not spare; he pours out my gall on the ground" (16:11-13).

Job traced his trial directly to God; after all, it was the Almighty who allowed the windstorm, the lightning, and the deaths of his children, livestock, and servants. It was the Lord who had allowed the devil to give Job painful sores all over his body. Certainly Satan was involved, but he was under the direct supervision and firm limitations imposed on him by God. Job realized that ultimately, all the calamity he had experienced had been permitted by God.

Finally, in the face of silence from heaven and the unending accusations of his friends, Job burst out in a soliloquy that revealed his sense of abandonment and despair. And yet he still was not without hope. He lamented his bitterness and his frustration at being unable to find God, yet he clung to his faith in the Lord and said, "But he knows the way that I take; when he has tried me, I shall come out as gold" (23:10).

If you are in despair—or perhaps someone you know is struggling mightily—pray even though it may seem God is indifferent. Be honest in the midst of disappointment with God's perceived lack of concern. Yet also rejoice in the assurance that He will restore you and make you stronger than ever, because "the tested genuineness of your faith—more precious than gold that perishes though it is tested by fire—may be found to result in praise and glory and honor at the revelation of Jesus Christ" (1 Peter 1:7).

A Prayer to Begin Your Time of Intercession

Father, I confess that many times I've been disappointed because it appears that You haven't answered my prayers and cries for help. Today, my need is great and specific, and I bring it to You again. Lord, help me to be content to say, "For your sake we are being killed all the day long; we are regarded as sheep to be slaughtered" (Romans 8:36). Give me the assurance that hardship is never to be interpreted as an abandonment of Your faithfulness.

I also pray that _____ might say with Job, "Though he slay me, I will hope in him" (Job 13:15). When they doubt, give them hope, and when they are in despair, give them comfort. Let not the self-righteous people who judge _____ hinder their faith in Your goodness and provision. And let grace and peace overwhelm them. Today, reveal Yourself to them that they might be able to pass the test of apparent abandonment, knowing that You are standing close to them even though they might not sense it.

In Jesus' name, Amen.

A Prayer That We Worship God in Our Trials

*"I know that you can do all things, and that no purpose of
yours can be thwarted. 'Who is this that hides counsel without
knowledge?' Therefore I have uttered what I did not understand,
things too wonderful for me, which I did not know...I had
heard of you by the hearing of the ear, but now my eye sees you;
therefore I despise myself, and repent in dust and ashes."*
—JOB 42:2-3,5,6

Last week, we saw Job's despair as he searched for God in the midst of his unforeseen trials. Yet he also persevered and saw the light of hope. No matter what happened, he would continue to believe and trust God.

After Job's friends ceased their moralizing, a young theologian by the name of Elihu showed up and rebuked Job for suggesting that God had been unjust or dealt with him unfairly.

Then God finally came on the scene and spoke to Job one on one, granting His servant's wish that he have opportunity to speak directly to the Almighty. However, rather than answering Job's questions, God responded with a few dozen questions of His own—questions about the created world, which Job could not answer. God's point: If you don't understand the created, physical realm, what makes you think that you can understand what I am doing in the moral realm? What makes you think you can understand My purposes for you or anyone else, for that matter?

Job was humiliated by this encounter. He had passed judgment on the Almighty, calling into question His justice and care for one of His servants. After God spoke, Job replied, "Behold, I am of small account;

what shall I answer you? I lay my hand on my mouth" (40:4). Having heard God, Job now realized that God's wisdom and justice were infinitely beyond human understanding. He also recognized that in the presence of God there is only one proper response: *worship*. And, as Job learned, we can worship God even when we don't understand what is going on.

Pray that all of us would be more consistent in our worship, knowing that God is beyond our understanding. Indeed, if we could "find Him out" and discern His hidden purposes, we would be bringing Him down to our level.

A Prayer to Begin Your Time of Intercession

Father, we worship You today. We confess that we have complained against You because life is often so hard for no apparent reason. We have questioned Your ways, believing that if we had Your power, we would have done a better job of running this universe than You've done.

Father, I pray for _____, that they might not rebel against Your sovereignty. I pray that when they see injustice in the world, they might not ascribe it to You. I pray that they might remember that You, O Lord, are God, and we are not. Help them to believe that Your way is perfect. And let that admission lead to submission, repentance, and thanksgiving.

In Jesus' name, Amen.

A Prayer That We Not Be Afraid

*"Fret not yourself because of evildoers; be not envious of wrong-doers! For they will soon fade like the grass and wither like the green herb. **Trust** in the LORD, and do good; dwell in the land and befriend faithfulness. **Delight** yourself in the LORD, and he will give you the desires of your heart. **Commit** your way to the LORD; trust in him, and he will act... **Be still** before the LORD and wait patiently for him."*

—PSALM 37:1-5,7 (emphasis added)

There are several commands in these verses that, if we were to obey them, we would find many heavy burdens lifted from our hearts. In this psalm, David was musing on a number of themes, always returning to the basic truth that we can trust God to come to our aid in His own time and in His own way. In short, God comes through for those who trust Him.

"Fret not," in the original Hebrew text, literally means "don't get heated." Then the commands follow: *trust, delight, commit* and *be still.* The bottom line is that we should change our focus from looking at our enemies and our fears to looking at God. We think, for example, of Stephen, who, when he was being stoned, gazed into heaven and God graciously gave him a vision of Jesus standing at His right hand. Stephen's last words were, "Lord, do not hold this sin against them" (Acts 7:60). Or we think of Paul and Silas in prison, not focused on their plight, but singing praises and praying late into the night (Acts 16:25). Consider a more contemporary example—that of Dietrich Bonhoeffer, who, before he was executed by hanging, was able to say, "This is the end—but for me, the beginning—of life."

What all these accounts have in common is this: Victorious believers have always been able to turn away from the threats of their enemies and focus their attention on God. As long as they gave praise and worship to God, they were able to withstand the attacks of their enemies— whether they were delivered, tortured, or even killed.

God gives us enemies because we need them. We need them to provoke us to a new level of worship and trust. We can't make our enemies go away, but we can dismiss them from our minds as we intentionally turn our focus to God, trust Him, and find in Him our delight.

Let us pray for ourselves and others that whether we are being attacked by our enemies, or by Satan himself, our focus would be on the worship of God. He is delighted when we look up to Him rather than at our enemies, who are encamped around us in an attempt to defeat our souls. I would encourage you to read all of Psalm 37 as a personal prayer for yourself and others.

A Prayer to Begin Your Time of Intercession

Father, I pray that You will help me to trust You and find delight in Your presence. Help me to be quiet and rest in You for as much time as is necessary to renew my confidence that You can be believed even when I am confronted by injustice and the threats of the wicked.

I pray for _____, who has been dismayed by those who have intentionally hurt them; I pray that they might not fret but deliberately turn their attention toward You. Let them know that "in your presence there is fullness of joy; at your right hand are pleasures forevermore" (Psalm 16:11). Today, become in their lives all that You can be for the glory of Your Son, Jesus.

In His name, Amen.

A Prayer That We Trust God Even in Calamity

"God is our refuge and strength, a very present help in trouble. Therefore we will not fear though the earth gives way, though the mountains be moved into the heart of the sea, though its waters roar and foam, though the mountains tremble at its swelling."

—PSALM 46:1-3

"'Be still, and know that I am God. I will be exalted among the nations, I will be exalted in the earth!' The LORD of hosts is with us; the God of Jacob is our fortress."

—PSALM 46:10-11

Katrina, Irene, and Sandy—these are the names of just three of the mighty hurricanes that have hit America's shores recently. This is not to mention the widespread devastation that has taken place in Haiti, Japan, and dozens of other countries in recent years as well, thanks to nature's fury.

When we turn the pages of the Bible, we discover that God is the One who openly takes responsibility for these disasters, even if He uses secondary causes—weather patterns, earth shifts, or even Satan—to do His bidding. Natural disasters are designed to teach us that life is often unexpectedly short, that eternity is more important than time, and that such disasters are a preview of much worse calamities still to come (Just read the book of Revelation!).

Of all the images that come to mind when I think back to the devastating earthquake in Haiti that killed more than 200,000 people, the one that has left the most indelible impression upon me is that of a young mother with a baby in her arms as she was being interviewed.

"I lost my son...he died in the rubble."

"Did you get to bury him?"

"No, no chance; his body was crushed in the rubble. I had to throw him away."

Then the news camera zeroed in on her backpack as she turned and prepared to board a bus. Stuffed in a side pocket was a Bible. As she boarded the bus she spoke to no one in particular, saying, "God is our refuge and strength, an ever-present help in trouble..." Her voice trailed off as she disappeared from view.

When the report was over, I kept staring at the television, pushing back tears and letting what I'd just seen sink into my soul. She had lost a child, she held a baby in her arms, and she was boarding a bus not knowing what she would do next. And yet there she was, still believing, still trusting that God is her refuge and strength.

Faith in adversity!

This mother—God bless her—began quoting Psalm 46 after she had finished the interview. This psalm was written as a praise song when God spared the city of Jerusalem from enemies who were threatening to annihilate the inhabitants. In the midst of a harrowing escape, the people found God to be an unshakable pillar. Please read the entire psalm for yourself.

Then pray for all those who today are experiencing calamities of whatever kind. Let us also pray for ourselves, that we would be able to trust God even when, humanly speaking, things do not make sense.

A Prayer to Begin Your Time of Intercession

Father, I pray that I might have the faith to trust You even when I experience devastating loss—whether it be my child, a loved one, or personal property. I pray that I would have the faith to believe that I belong to You and You will care for me, and that is all that really matters because time is short and eternity is long.

I pray for _____, that they might trust You in the midst of their loss. I pray that when their faith fails, You will grant them the strength and the comfort to believe that Your promises are still true. I pray they will realize that Your care for them is not dependent on a good outcome in this world, but that You will carry them victoriously to our heavenly home.

Strengthen our faith, Lord, for we are weak.

In Jesus' name, Amen.

A Prayer That God's Word Would Penetrate Our Hearts

"The word of God is living and active, sharper than any two-edged sword, piercing to the division of soul and of spirit, of joints and of marrow, and discerning the thoughts and intentions of the heart. And no creature is hidden from his sight, but all are naked and exposed to the eyes of him to whom we must give account."

—HEBREWS 4:12-13

We should not be surprised that the Word of God is compared to a sword. A Roman sword had two edges; it cut both ways. God does not use the sword of the Word to destroy His people, but rather to wound them that He might heal them. In fact, the word "sharper" in Hebrews 4:12 is from a word that means "to cut." It is the language of surgery, the language of dissection. The Word of God does not *divide* the soul from the spirit, but rather it *penetrates* both soul and spirit. In brief, it goes to the heart of what and who we are—it lays us bare. In the presence of the Word of God, there is no pretense.

Consider other characteristics of the Word of God:

First, it is "living and active." That is, it actually has power; it converts the soul. We are born again "not of perishable seed but of imperishable, through the living and abiding word of God" (1 Peter 1:23). When the Word of God acts, God acts.

Second, the Word of God discerns "the thoughts and intentions of the heart." It sits in judgment on all the activities of the soul and spirit; it judges all our thoughts and reflections. The Bible monitors the thousands of thoughts that flow through our minds each day; even our "intentions" are judged. Greek scholar Kenneth Wuest translated this last phrase as saying that the Word of God is "the sifter and analyzer of the reflections and conceptions of the heart." [11]

Third, we read, "No creature is hidden from his sight, but all are naked and exposed to the eyes of him to whom we must give account." The imagery is of a corpse laid on a table with every sinew, every nerve, and every particle of flesh laid bare. Like an X-ray machine, the Word of God reveals who we are. Christ examines the plates carefully, noting every speck and determining whether it's healthy or sick.

The Word of God penetrates our psychic radar systems and breaks our defense mechanisms, exposing our self-delusions and rationalizations. If we are open to receiving its message, it is God's power to us. Let us pray that His Word would cut deeply into our hearts, both to expose our sin that we might confess it, and to bring the healing and help we all desire.

A Prayer to Begin Your Time of Intercession

Father, forgive me for neglecting Your Word; forgive me for the times I've tried to live off of substitutes. May I be able to say, "I have stored up your word in my heart, that I might not sin against you" (Psalm 119:11). I've learned that the more I meditate on Your Word, the greater my appetite for it; the more I neglect it, the less I miss it. Let me begin today with a new resolve to "meditate on it day and night" (Joshua 1:8). Give me a hunger that can only be satisfied by Your Word.

And now I pray for _____, that they might not be like the person who hears the Word then walks away, but rather like those who are "doers of the word, and not hearers only" (James 1:22). Keep them from the deception of thinking that because they have heard Your Word, they've done it; keep them from confusing *hearing* with *doing*.

May Your Word be like a hammer that breaks the rock in pieces, so to speak. Let the seeds sown in their hearts bear the fruit of holy desire—namely, a love for Your Word and a willingness to hear You speak. Today, cause them to submit to Your Word.

In Jesus' name, Amen.

A Prayer That We Draw Near to God with Confidence

"Therefore, brothers, since we have confidence to enter the holy
places by the blood of Jesus, by the new and living way that he
opened for us through the curtain, that is, through his flesh, and
since we have a great priest over the house of God, let us draw
near with a true heart in full assurance of faith, with our
hearts sprinkled clean from an evil conscience..."

—HEBREWS 10:19-22

Once a year, the Old Testament high priests entered the Holy Place in the Jerusalem temple and went behind the curtain into the Holy of Holies to sprinkle blood on the Ark of the Covenant, making intercession to God for themselves and the people.

Tradition says that a rope was tied around the high priest's lower leg so that if it should happen he died inside the Holy of Holies (perhaps because he failed to heed God's exact instructions), he could be pulled from behind the curtain without anyone needing to enter the sacred place. Although God dwells everywhere, this small room was where God's presence was localized.

When Jesus died on the cross, the veil that guarded the Holy of Holies—that is, the curtain that separated the people from God's presence—was ripped down the middle, from top to bottom. This torn veil symbolized that a new era had come, and that entrance into the Holy of Holies was accessible to anyone who would enter through the shed blood of Christ. Even better, Christ actually "brought us to God," as it were; we are now in the Holy of Holies, the very citadel of God's presence.

We read that we have complete assurance that we can now enter into the holy place; we don't have to draw back in fear. Rather, we can come with boldness and know that we are invited, welcomed, and heard. Here we meet one-on-one with the Almighty.

Earlier, I emphasized that the purpose of prayer is not simply to have our requests heard and answered according to God's will, but also to enjoy God's presence. In our rushed world, we've forgotten that communion with God is not simply a verbal connection; it's a *relational* one.

This week, rather than spending a lot of time asking God for this or that, won't you spend time in His presence, enjoying His favor? We are assured, "In your presence there is fullness of joy" (Psalm 16:11).

Jesus brought us into the Holy of Holies not only so we could address our sin issues and personal needs, but so we might also enter with confidence into God's presence to cultivate our growing relationship with Him.

A Prayer to Begin Your Time of Intercession

Father, I thank You that I am in Your presence being heard and received. I thank You that the Most Holy Place that was so inaccessible in Old Testament times is now open to me, and that I can enter by the blood of Jesus. I rejoice that even as I sorrow over my sin—however dark and regrettable it is—You and I can meet for fellowship and reconciliation. Through Jesus I am made acceptable; through Him my sin is cleansed and fellowship with You is restored. Teach me to enjoy Your presence.

Now, Lord, I pray for _____, that they might know that if they come to You by way of Christ, they will be welcomed and received, forgiven and set free. Cause them to see that the path has been cleared, and that they do not have to be Your permanent enemy. Help them to know that You don't have Your back toward them, but rather You're there with arms outstretched to welcome them into Your presence. May they know that the issue is not the greatness of their sin, but rather the great value of the blood that was shed for them. Bring deliverance and hope into their hearts.

In Jesus' name, Amen.

A Prayer That We Anticipate Christ's Return

"Behold, he is coming with the clouds, and every eye will see him, even those who pierced him, and all tribes of the earth will wail on account of him. Even so. Amen."

—REVELATION 1:7

"Since all these things are thus to be dissolved, what sort of people ought you to be in lives of holiness and godliness, waiting for and hastening the coming of the day of God, because of which the heavens will be set on fire and dissolved, and the heavenly bodies will melt as they burn!"

—2 PETER 3:11-12

The purpose of prophecy is not to satisfy our curiosity about the future but rather to change our attitudes about this life and the next. The return of Christ is always presented in Scripture as a motivation for holy living, and to remind us that it's not necessary for us to win in this life in order to win in the life to come. In other words, the return of Jesus assures us that (1) we will be reunited with our loved ones; (2) the injustices done on earth will finally be answered and resolved; and most importantly, (3) we will all be in the presence of God the Father, the Son, and the Holy Spirit forever.

On July 4, 1952, 34-year-old Florence Chadwick waded into the water at Catalina Island hoping to be the first woman to swim the 21-mile strait to California. The water was numbing cold, and the fog was so thick that she couldn't even see the boats in her own party. As the hours ticked by she swam on, but 15 hours later, numbed by the cold, she asked to be taken out of the water. Within a few minutes, the small party realized that they were about half a mile from the shore. Florence regretted having given up, by saying, "If only I would have been able to see the shore, I could have made it."

Two years later Florence made another attempt. Although the weather was the same, this time she succeeded. The reason? She said this time around, she kept the image of the shoreline in her mind.

We can endure a great deal of what comes our way in life when we "keep the image of the shoreline" in our minds and hearts. The certainty of the return of Jesus motivates us to endure, whether the water is smooth or rough. Eternity will rectify what time seemed to ruin; it is the sure knowledge that we will land safely on the shore that matters. We have read the last chapter, and we know the story will end well!

A Prayer to Begin Your Time of Intercession

Father, I pray that You will help me to be motivated by the sure knowledge that Jesus will return again. Cause me to live a pure life of holiness and anticipate Your coming. I pray that I would live this week as if I knew for sure that You were coming by next weekend. Let me be a witness to Your saving grace in the lives of those who are not ready for Your return.

And now, Father, I pray for _____, that they might also be aware that life is short, and that they will either meet You in death or perhaps live to see Your return. I pray that they might love Jesus so much that they would look forward to seeing Him return. If they do not know You as Savior, turn their hearts in Your direction; give them a sense of their own personal need and capture their hearts for Your glory and honor.

In Jesus' name, Amen.

A Prayer of Thanks to God for His Victory

*"Then the seventh angel blew his trumpet, and there were loud
voices in heaven, saying, 'The kingdom of the world has become
the kingdom of our Lord and of his Christ, and he shall reign
forever and ever.' And the twenty-four elders who sit on their
thrones before God fell on their faces and worshiped God, saying,
'We give thanks to you, Lord God Almighty, who is and who
was, for you have taken your great power and begun to reign.
The nations raged, but your wrath came, and
the time for the dead to be judged, and for rewarding your
servants, the prophets and saints, and those who fear
your name, both small and great, and for destroying the
destroyers of the earth.'"*
—REVELATION 11:15-18

*"They have conquered him by the blood of the Lamb
and by the word of their testimony, for they loved
not their lives even unto death."*
—REVELATION 12:11

Notice in the first passage above that the word "kingdom" is singular, reminding us that all the diverse individual kingdoms of this world, comprising various countries, nationalities, and cultures, are really under the domain of one leader, and that's Satan. But this kingdom, in all of its various forms, will ultimately become the kingdom of the Lord Jesus Christ. There will be no place in the entire universe—including hell—where Jesus does not reign. All things shall be put under His feet.

The 24 elders, who probably represent the 12 apostles and the 12 tribes of Israel (thus representing the raptured church and Old Testament saints), appropriately fall on their faces and worship before the throne. Their praise is focused on God's sovereignty—His irresistible power; no one can thwart His plans and purposes. He exists from eternity to eternity. He always was, He presently is, and He always will be to come. Given His uncontested rule over the earth, it's only appropriate that He be worshipped without reservation or questions.

The reign of God on earth will not be welcomed by everyone. Satan, for example, is enraged with the knowledge that his kingdom will eventually have to be surrendered to the Lord Jesus Christ. In an event that probably takes place during the Great Tribulation, we find that Satan will be thrown out of heaven by the angelic forces led by Michael. And although Satan will be very angry and do as much damage as he can, in the end, he will be defeated and thrown into the lake of fire.

How can we prepare for heaven while we are still on earth? The answer is to learn heaven's songs of gratitude and praise, and sing them often! All through eternity, we will be giving God the praise He so richly deserves, and we can practice doing this right now. Yes, we will serve Him in many different ways when we're in heaven, but praise will always take center stage in the presence of the eternal King. So we may as well make praise an active part of our lives today.

So let us pray, preparing for heaven:

Father, I join with the saints and all creatures in heaven to give You praise, for You have always been, You are now, and You will always be. I anticipate the day when Jesus will begin His sovereign reign on earth. I'm grateful that You, O Lord, have invited us to the celebration, and I gladly accept. Let my entire life be one of praise and gratitude, and may I express this to You often, with spontaneous joy and heartfelt wonder.

I pray for _____, that they might live each day with an attitude of praise and personal appreciation for Your grace and power. I pray that they might be caught up in the wonder of Your salvation on our behalf, and that they might rejoice in Your attributes of infinite wisdom, mercy, and sovereignty. Cause them—indeed, cause all of us—to never neglect daily, intentional, and heartfelt praise. Teach us to bring heaven down to earth by joining the chorus of those who are already in Your presence giving You the adoration that You deserve. In Jesus' name, Amen.

A Prayer That We Be Sure of Our Salvation

"If anyone's name was not found written in the book of life, he was thrown into the lake of fire."
—REVELATION 20:15

"And night will be no more. They will need no light of lamp or sun, for the Lord God will be their light, and they will reign forever and ever."
—REVELATION 22:5

The contrast between an eternal hell and an eternal heaven could not be more vivid, more motivating, and above all, more frightening. When I read these passages, I ask myself: Where are the people who are too good to go to hell, but not good enough to go to heaven? Surely there is some middle ground, some eternal purgatory where the vast majority of decent but unconverted humanity will reside.

But there is no such place. The Bible paints reality like it is: either eternal torment or eternal bliss. "Every human being," said C.S. Lewis, "is in the process of becoming a noble being; noble beyond imagination. Or else, alas, a vile being beyond redemption." Lewis exhorts us to remember that "the dullest and most uninteresting person you can talk to may one day be a creature which, if you saw it now, you would be strongly tempted to worship, or else a horror and a corruption such as you now meet, if at all only in a nightmare…There are no ordinary people…it is immortals whom we joke with, work with, marry and snub and exploit—immortal horrors or everlasting splendors."[12]

Imagine for a moment hordes of people resurrected to appear at the Great White Throne Judgment. We are struck with their diversity:

the pauper stands next to the multibillionaire, and the servant stands next to the king. All religions are well represented, as are all continents and countries. This vast multitude is united in this: Each person lacks the one thing needed to stand in the presence of a holy God; each one lacks the righteousness of Christ that can shield them from God's anger and righteous judgments.

Meanwhile, the redeemed have an entirely different destiny. They behold God directly, without a mediator and without sin coming in between to hinder their fellowship with the Almighty. Theirs is a destiny of uninterrupted joy, unending relationships, and eternal bliss.

The stark contrast between these groups has to do with whether a person has a relationship to Jesus. The apostle Peter urged us to "confirm your calling and election" (2 Peter 1:10). Those who end up in heaven will be those who believe that when Christ died for sinners, He did all that will ever be necessary to save us. Those who transfer their trust to Christ will be saved, and they'll know it. Thus, salvation is based on the promises of God and the witness of the Holy Spirit.

Let us use this prayer time to ask God to search our hearts in order to make sure that we have confidence that we belong to Him, and to pray for those who might be self-deceived, believing themselves to be saved when, in actuality, they are not.

A Prayer to Begin Your Time of Intercession

Father, I call out to You today, first of all, that You might give me renewed confidence that I do belong to You—that I am Your child through faith in Jesus Christ. Give me the assurance that will make me bold in my witness, and willing, if need be, to die for Christ, knowing that my eternal destiny is secure. May this confidence cause me to rejoice in Your wonderful salvation.

And now I pray for _____, that they also might have the assurance that they belong to You. I pray that You will reveal to them whether their faith is real or whether they are self-deceived. I am reminded of those who will someday say, "Lord, Lord" and then list the miracles You have done, and yet You will reply, "I never knew you; depart from me, you workers of lawlessness" (Matthew 7:23).

Lord, I plead for _____, that they might not only be saved, but be assured of it through Your promises and the witness of the Holy Spirit.

In Jesus' name, Amen.

Notes

1. Daniel Henderson, *Transforming Prayer* (Minneaplis: Bethany, 2011), 48.

2. Source not found, but similar challenges of the relationship between God's love for us and our own predicaments are found in Larry Crabb, *The Papa Prayer* (Nashville: Thomas Nelson, 2006), 101-10.

3. Jerry Bridges, *Trusting God* (Colorado Springs: NavPress, 1990), 155.

4. C.H. Spurgeon, "A Mystery! Saints Sorrowing and Jesus Glad!" A sermon preached on Sunday morning, August 7, 1864, http://www.spurgeon .org/sermons/0585.htm.

5. "O Love That Wilt Not Let Me Go," by George Matheson, 1882.

6. William Cowper, "O for a Closer Walk with God," 1772.

7. David Bryant, *Christ Is All!* (New Providence, NJ: New Providence Publishers, 2003), 19.

8. John MacArthur, *The MacArthur New Testament Commentary—Galatians* (Chicago: Moody, 1987), 60.

9. D.A. Carson, *A Call to Spiritual Reformation: Priorities from Paul and His Prayers* (Grand Rapids: Baker, 1992), 187.

10. Robert Munger, *My Heart—Christ's Home* (Downers Grove, IL: InterVarsity, 1992).

11. Kenneth Wuest, *Hebrews in the Greek New Testament* (Grand Rapids: Eerdmans, 1948), 89.

12. C.S.Lewis, "The Weight of Glory" in *The Weight of Glory and Other Addresses*, rev. and exp. ed. (New York: Macmillan, 1980), 18-19.

Other Good Harvest House Reading
by Erwin W. Lutzer and Rebecca Lutzer

Life-Changing Bible Verses You Should Know
Erwin W. Lutzer & Rebecca Lutzer

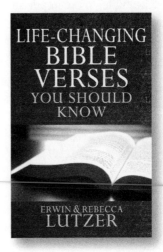

After Erwin and Rebecca Lutzer realized that memorizing Scripture has nearly become a lost pursuit today, they decided to create this practical, relevant resource filled with powerful verses and insightful explanations to help stimulate a spiritual hunger in every believer's life. With more than 35 topics and questions for reflection and further study, you'll discover how God's Word will...

- sustain you in times of need
- comfort you in seasons of sorrow
- strengthen your heart in times and areas of weakness
- direct your steps and decisions toward God's will

These handpicked verses provide a foundation of wisdom and hope that will show you who God is and what He has done for you, as well as how you can successfully live the Christian life.

Awesome Bible Verses Every Kid Should Know

Rebecca Lutzer

Now children ages 7 to 12 can enjoy the Bible's most important passages in a fun and engaging format. Each two-page spread features a few verses set in an appealing "Bible" graphic, a brief explanation and application, and open-ended questions adults can use to help kids talk about their faith.

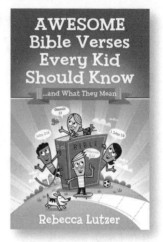

On the Path with God

Erwin W. Lutzer

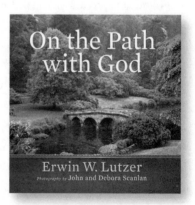

Inspiring meditations join breathtaking photographs of winding country paths and cobblestone streets and invite you to take time to walk with God. The joy-filled promises of faith in this book await anyone who treasures an enriched journey with the Creator.

The Cross in the Shadow of the Crescent
Erwin W. Lutzer

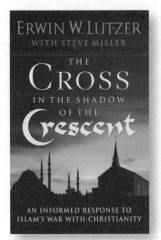

Islam is on the rise all over the West, including in America. This book urges Christians to see this as both a reason for concern and an opportunity to share the gospel, and tackles the key questions people are asking:

- What agenda do Islamists have for the West?
- How might Islam's growing influence affect me personally?
- What should the church be doing in response?

A sensitive and highly informative must-read!